THE ART OF BUDGETING

MONEY MATTERS MONDAYS | BUILDING KINGDOM WEALTH

VOLUME 1

HENRIETTA ENGLAND

Edited by

NICOLE QUEEN

VISION PUBLISHING HOUSE

Vision Publishing House
www.vision-publishinghouse.com

ISBN: 978-1-955297-32-5 (Paperback)

"The world we have created is a product of our thinking; it cannot be changed without changing our thinking."

— ALBERT EINSTEIN

CONTENTS

A WORD FROM THE AUTHOR

In today's society, we see that most people expect a right-now fix, a right-now turnaround. It can happen suddenly, but are you prepared for the abundance? Abundance is receiving large quantities of something, plentifulness of the good things in life, and prosperity. God desires to give to us according to the measure of our faith and belief. To receive, one must be prepared and ready for the increase and overflow in every area of life.

Life is a journey. We will make mistakes. We will do things that we thought we would never do. We will fall from grace. It is not about how we failed. It's not about how many mistakes we have made. It's about: *Where do we go from here?* Therefore, we should ask ourselves: *How can I learn from my mistakes? What lesson can I take away from the mistakes? What can I do differently? How can I change my old habits and learn new skills to apply to my everyday life?*

Every failure in life is an opportunity for a new beginning—
begin again and start afresh.

In this book, you will be encouraged to gain control over your household budget, and learn how to make strategic decisions regarding your finances, while learning that money is a tool to be used to advance your life and lifestyle. Money is not your boss; instead, you are the boss of your money. You will command your money to go, do, and bring back a harvest of much fruit.

Now, to accomplish increase, abundance, overflow, and prosperity, one must learn discipline in every area of life and in every circumstance. Speak life to every dead situation. Speak increase and apply the principles and precepts being taught to advance your life and the life of those you hold near and dear to your heart. There is a right way and a wrong way to bring increase. Increase comes with consistency, repetition, and due diligence in all financial matters concerning your life and the legacy you choose to leave in the earth. Debt is a choice!

> *Let no debt remain outstanding, except the continuing debt to love one another, for whoever loves others has fulfilled the law.*
>
> — ROMANS 13:8 NIV

Love is the debt we carry. To be rich in love is to live in full alignment with the command of God. God will see our good works and our faith; He will establish the works of our hands. Preparation is key to unlocking and locking financial opportunities both now and for the future of our offspring, for generations to come.

So, come journey with us to financial freedom. Be sure to purchase our official companion journal, *The Art of Budgeting: The Journey to Financial Freedom Journal,* to excel in fiscal fitness.

WHO WE ARE: TRI-FOLD CONNECTIONS

Tri-Fold Connection's mission is to prepare everyone (regardless of race, creed, color, age, culture, religion, or denomination) for an abundant life. We do this by changing the mindset to be prepared, to acquire new skills in financial stability, and to create kingdom wealth, God's way.

We empower our clients with Biblical principles, precepts, and encouragement to achieve their goals, dreams, visions, and assignments. We coach you to effectively use your time, talent, and treasures to work for you to live life the way God intended in abundance, overflow, and prosperity.

We aspire to educate adolescents, young adults, adults, seniors, and people with disabilities on economic growth and development and creditworthiness, with our primary focus on financial literacy. Our motto is fiscal fitness, and our goal is for you to have a transformation lasting a lifetime™.

We desire to become your accountability coach, partner with you, and help you to design success for you and your legacy. We offer a variety of services, and your initial consultation is free.

Contact us via:
Website: www.trifoldconnectionsllc.com
Email: info@trifoldconnectionsllc.com
Phone: 708-553-0002

Scan below to access your free gift (Budget Planning for Ownership Worksheet) or visit my website.

BUDGET WORKSHEET

TRI FOLD CONNECTIONS

1

KNOW WHERE YOU STAND FINANCIALLY

One of the most important steps to financial freedom is making a list of all that you own, all that you owe, and all that you earn. This is called keeping records! It's the principle of accounting and the beginning of creating a budget/ balance sheet. Your expenses subtracted from your income equals available surplus (cash-on-hand). Your liabilities subtracted from your assets equals capital (liquid cash).

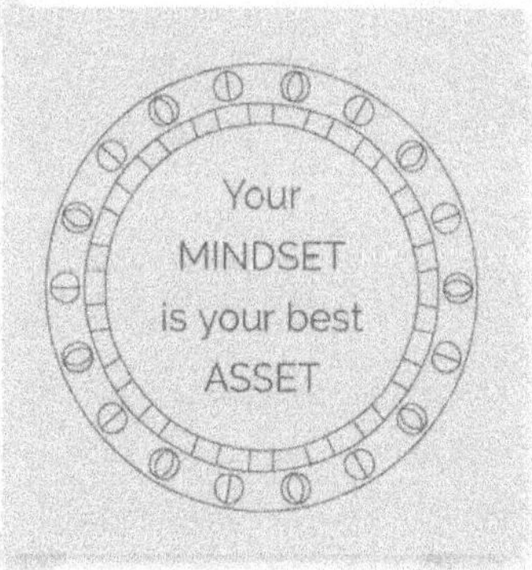

The Bible says, "By wisdom a house is built, and through understanding it is established" (Proverbs 24:3 NIV). You are wise with your money when you know where it is, where it's going, and where it's coming from.

People like to use the term "money talks." Money doesn't talk! It just walks away quietly. Let's say you get to the end of the month and ask, "Where did my money go?" It means you are not keeping a proper budget. When you have a budget, you are telling your money where you want it to go rather than wondering where it went.

A Budget Is Simply a Planned Activity

A budget is simply *planned spending*. A budget holds you accountable to save for the things you need, instead of only buying the things you want. A budget is essential for you to become a great money manager.

Why is it important to keep good records and know what you owe, earn, and own? It is because ignorance plus easy credit equals disaster. It's a sure recipe for disaster!

When I enter a store, I leave my credit cards at home. If I don't know whether I can afford it or not, I am already in trouble. It's immature to decide before knowing the facts. It's also unwise to buy something before you know if you can afford it. The only way to know where you stand with your finances is by keeping good records and budgeting your spending.

Another translation of Proverbs 24:3 says, "Any enterprise is built by wise planning, becomes strong through common sense, and profits wonderfully by keeping abreast of the facts" (TLB). Make your list, know the facts of your financial situation, and live accordingly. A different translation of Proverbs 24:3 says, "It takes wisdom to build a house, and understanding to set it on a firm foundation; It takes knowledge to furnish its rooms with fine furniture and beautiful draperies" (MSG).

Types of Income - The Life Curve

The life curve is volatile, which means it's moving consistently. This curve starts with accumulation. If you are not wise, you will look up and realize that you do not have any investments or savings to fall back on during retirement. Thus, when you begin working, you must also begin saving and investing in your future. Search out different avenues or instruments for saving that work for you. You learn with self-discipline to turn your income into assets, and assets equal liquid cash-on-hand. At the top of the life curve, there is retirement. As consumers, we want our investments to be in real estate, stocks, bonds, dividends, 401K, Certificate of Deposit (CD), annuities, and Individual Retirement Account (IRA). We want these investments to work for us and provide liquid assets by retirement.

Another type of income that can build your assets is a whole life insurance policy. This policy builds cash value over time and can be used for pulling money or assets needed versus pulling your funds from the stock market altogether. Your goal is to accumulate as many assets as possible during your working years, meaning you must exercise self-discipline and self-control. It's easy to get caught up in the latest fashion and technology gadgets, but if I'm honest, these things change rapidly. So, if we are not budgeting or being accountable, we can quickly find ourselves upside down financially. The world is always in our eyes and ear gates through advertisements on television, Google, Facebook, YouTube, and other social media outlets. These advertisements tell us how affordable and necessary things are to entice us to purchase them.

On the downward side of the life curve, there is a distribution. This is where your income becomes assets, and it is now "working for you," meaning you are receiving monthly dividend disbursement from your investments. The investment now pays you in monthly income, which adds to your gross monthly/ annual income. This directly affects your budget and buying power. This also includes real estate that you have invested in for rental; if it is paid in full, the rental is considered income, which is free and clear of a mortgage. (Remember, rental income is only estimated at 75% of income received from rental. Why? This is because with rental property, there must be an escrow fund for unexpected repairs and expenses).

Three Steps to Deal with Stress

1. Decide! Make a decision! Cut away the fat! Move beyond your comfort zone and perceived limitations with a firm decision to grow bigger than the sources of your stress.

2. Trust God! Trusting God is foundational, and it will give you the confidence needed to grow beyond your challenges. God will build your life, step-by-step. He will make a way when there is no way.

3. Speak words of life! A generous confession focuses on the positive, and faith-filled expectations that will move your life forward. Be intentional with your words. The carnal nature (relating to physical, especially sexual, needs, and activities) always defaults to the negative.

God has big plans for you, but you won't fulfill them if you stay small-minded. You no longer experience distress when your capacity increases. Developing your capacity is an ongoing journey that yields a fulfilling life. Starting from the beginning is a good place to start, and the beginning of financial freedom is budgeting. Planning and investing in oneself are like golden nuggets when building kingdom wealth. The goal is to build a complete financial portfolio; and although we are faced with uncertainty during these times, we can still take steps to grow our financial literacy and financial portfolio.

Prayer of Thanksgiving

Thank You, God, for being all-wise and all-knowing. The Holy Spirit walks with me, leading and guiding me in life, health, and strength. He gives me the wisdom to create wealth. Thank You, God, that your blessing will overtake me and my household. God, shower down Your blessing upon us – blessings of wisdom, knowledge, clear understanding, wise counsel, simple trust, and healing. God, we need You and can do nothing without You.

Lord, help us to build solid-lasting relationships. We desire to have an intimate relationship with You and to commune with You. You are welcome to come in and take over our lives.

Thank You, God, for we no longer walk in darkness, but have Your divine light to light our path to go before us. May anything that is not of You be removed for the path to be made straight.

Oh, God, let your light shine in us and through us. As we go about our day, we put on the full armor of God so that we may be able to withstand evil and wickedness. Every day, we put on our loins girt about with truth; our breastplate of righteousness (right living before God); our feet shod with the preparation of the gospel of peace; and above all, our shield of faith, that we may be able to quench all the fiery darts of the wicked ones. We also take the helmet of salvation and the sword of the Spirit (the Word or Logos of God).

> *"Praying always with all prayer and supplications in the Spirit, and watching thereunto, with all perseverance and supplications for all saints." — Ephesians 6:18 KJV*

God, cover us today and keep Your words hidden in our hearts so that we may not sin against Thee. Let these words I speak be a light to someone's path and a lamp to guide them through these difficult financial times. May You open the ears to hear and receive, the eyes to see, and the hearts to transform and be renewed by Your Word and Your ways. May these principles and precepts be applied to our lives daily. Lord, give us the courage and the boldness to step outside of what is safe, comfortable, and familiar as we trust You to cover us with your all-sufficient grace and mercy.

Holy Spirit, teach us how to grow our capacity to handle life's challenges from a posture of trust and expectation of good. Thank You, God, for Your faithfulness to us, even when we don't see it. You are our refuge and our strength. And with You, God, all things are possible!

In Jesus' mighty Authority, we pray. Amen.

* * *

2

CONSIDER YOUR DEBT AND CREATE A BUDGET

First Corinthians 4:14-16 was written by Paul; he was talking to the Believers at the Church of Corinth. He wanted to encourage the Believers to be servants of God. Paul reminded the Believers in Corinth: "Yes, I am a leader, but think of me as a servant of God." When we realize we are servants of God (not man), we are more willing to release our control over to God. We must allow God to control every area of our lives, even our finances. Paul also shared with the believers of Corinth that he, too, was not asking them to do anything that he had not done himself.

> "I'm not writing all this as a neighborhood scold to shame you. I'm writing as a father to you, my children. I love you and want you to grow up well, not spoiled. There are a lot of people around who can't wait to tell you what you've done wrong, but there aren't many fathers willing to take the time and effort to help you grow up. It was as Jesus helped me proclaim God's Message to you that I became your

> father. I'm not, you know, asking you to do anything I'm not already doing myself.
>
> — 1 CORINTHIANS 4:14-16 (MSG)

I, Henrietta England, am not asking you to do something that I have not done, myself. And to this very day, I still do. I pay off debt, save money weekly, invest in my retirement, set up an inheritance for my children's children, save for vacations, create a monthly budget, pay my tithes and offerings, give to the less fortunate, provide for the orphans and widows, and sow seeds into the good grown.

Just as we want a financial planner to manage our money well, God wants us to manage His money well. The ability to manage our money well is a skill that many of us grew up not learning. Budgeting was not a roundtable discussion at the dinner table, but learning this valuable skill is key to our success. Managing our money is vital to a happy and complete life. We must get out of fear or embarrassment and ask for the help we need. We must learn new skills that can change the rest of our lives. Being a good money manager simply means to be cautious of our spending habits and aware of how much money we are spending.

What Is A Budget?

A budget is a tool to help you manage your money. Your budget shows you where your money is coming from and going. It's where you are spending your money versus the income you have coming in. A budget holds you accountable and keeps you responsible for your spending habits. Therefore, you can save for the things you need, instead of buying only the things you want.

Many people hear the word budget and cringe like it's taboo. A budget is essential for you and I in becoming great money managers of our empire and/or enterprise. We must learn to use discretion when spending our hard-earned income. Discretions refer to judgment and decision-making, in which you must determine how to go about a process in a proper and fitting way. Additionally, it refers to having discernment (or good judgment) and making responsible decisions. After you have utilized discretion, you must make some decisions. According to the website "SchoolCounselor.org," a decision is "a conclusion or resolution reached after consideration; it is also "the action or process of deciding something or of resolving a question." It also means to cut something or the process of making a choice after careful consideration. When making a budget, you must decide what your needs versus what your wants are.

Needs vs. Wants

> "The good person is generous and lends lavishly; no shuffling or stumbling around for this one, But a sterling and solid and lasting reputation."
>
> — PSALM 112:5-6 (MSG)

If we are honest with ourselves, what we want isn't what we need in most cases. To be honest, we know we have been given far more than we actually need. Life can be tricky in that way. Our minds are likened to a computer's hard drive. It processes thousands of pictures, sounds, and directives, daily. No wonder we feel overloaded and become disconnected. We truly need only a few things, and all the other things are wants or desires. Our true needs are food, water, clothing, shelter, and financial resources. We want everything else, like cars, to be socially accepted by our peers or into a particular group. We go out and buy shoes, clothes, and handbags. We make reservations at five-star hotels and go on lavish vacations. We want VIP status at clubs, bars, and restaurants; bottle service which starts at $100; the latest "drip," hairstyles, and make-up; spa treatment; and plastic surgery. These are just a few examples of things we desire rather than what we actually need.

So, how do you find joy when you can't get what you want? Contentment is contingent on your attitude, not your bank account/statement. If you are always looking to make more money, gain more resources, or acquire more wealth for yourself, you are not using money how God designed it to be used.

Money Is a Tool

Money is a tool to be used for your benefit. There are three ways in which money can be a tool:

1. Money is to provide for your needs.
2. Money is to provide for the needs of others.
3. Money is an opportunity to give back to God as an act of worship.

In the section above, we established that money provides for our needs. Those needs are food, water, clothing, shelter, and financial resources. When properly preparing a budget (whether it be weekly, bi-weekly, monthly, or quarterly), your needs must come first. For a healthy body, you need proper nutrition. This is important, especially in these modern times, when the health crisis has become a part of our everyday consciousness. Your body is made up of two-thirds water, and it's a no-brainer how important water is for hydration and the removal of impurities in your body. In addition, water helps maintain healthy skin and healthy hair, while also giving you relief from fatigue. These are just a few of the many benefits water can provide.

Money is a tool to provide for those who are in need, widowed, or orphaned. At times, even those who have done well in life can fall short and require assistance. There are also times where we must help those who are parentless or widowed. The Bible says, "Look after orphans and widows in their distress" (James 1:27 NIV). Let's face it, we are all connected in one way or the other. When one member of the body is hurting, the entire body is hurting (1 Corinthians 12: 25-26 NIV). It would be a better environment here on Earth if we exercise this principle of being one in the body.

By giving to God, you are declaring your satisfaction is not money but Jesus! Jesus is the one who provides for you and your household. Worshiping and loving money more than God leads to:

- Pain
- Let Downs
- Depression
- Sin
- Anxiety
- Betrayal/ Deceit

Trust God to provide for your needs, and you will find contentment there. Your money may run out, but God is a generous giver, who is with you and for you, through every situation, no matter what. God is our ride-or-die!

If we're being honest, we all have depended on others and have been let down by individuals who have said one thing and did the total opposite of what they promised us. When we trust God and obey Him with our money and lives, we receive His rich love and the transformation it creates within us – a transformation that lasts a lifetime™.

> "You can be sure that God will take care of everything you need, his generosity exceeding even yours in glory that pours from Jesus. Our God and Father abounds in glory that just pours out into eternity. Yes."
>
> — PHILIPPIANS 4:19-20 (MSG)

> "A devout life does bring wealth, but it's the rich simplicity of being yourself before God. Since we enter the world penniless and will leave it penniless, if we have bread on the table and shoes on our feet, that's enough. But if it's only money these leaders are after, they'll self-destruct in no time. Lust for money brings trouble and nothing but trouble. Going down

> that path, some lose their footing in the faith completely and live to regret it bitterly ever after."
>
> — 1 TIMOTHY 6:6-10 (MSG)

Prayer of Stewardship

Father God, we come to you today to thank You for being a God of another chance. We thank You for our lives, having our right minds, the activity of our limbs, and our hearts pumping the blood and oxygen we need to move, live, and breathe.

Thank You, God, for sweet rest— resting in Your presence, knowing everything will be alright, trusting that You will do just what You said. Your word cannot return back void, so the very words You have spoken must come to pass. We thank You for allowing us to make good, sound decisions in our lives. We thank You for providing for every one of our needs. We thank You for giving us all blessings, overflow, and abundance.

Help us, God, to be better stewards over our financial matters. Help us to understand that You provide all our needs— houses, cars, vacations, meals, and clothes. God, You are Jehovah Jireh, our Provider. Jesus, You have entrusted us with so much. Help us to manage our money well. Help us to stay committed to our budgets and savings plans we have put in place.

Thank you, Jesus, for always having our best interests at heart. Help us to be content in You and You alone. Lord, give us wisdom for wisdom comes from You. Lord, help us to cut away the things we desire and want. Help us be content with what we have for you alone, God, supply every one of our needs.

Father God, we thank You for our ability to live in freedom. Help us to be better servants to You, oh God. You alone, God, fill the longings of our hearts. Give us the courage to live in freedom instead of returning to our old vices.

Help us stay FOCUSed (Following One Course Until Successful). God, You said You would bless us according to our faith. So, God, I ask that You help us in our unbelief. Increase our faith. Increase our wisdom. Increase our knowledge and understanding of your Word.

Help us exercise self-control and self-discipline, keeping us humble and meek—not boasting about ourselves, but on Your great and mighty works in our lives.

Father God, we thank You for preparing us to walk in Your wealthy place—
Your place of abundance and overflow.
We thank You for Your daily favor, grace, and new mercies.

God, we close this prayer and seal it in the mighty Name of Jesus. We bind up any attack of the enemy to steal or distort this prayer. I bind up any retaliatory demons that would try to steal this word.

Now come, Holy Spirit. You are welcome to come and sup with us on this day.
We ask these prayers and the unspoken prayers of our hearts today.

In Jesus' mighty Name, we pray. Amen.

* * *

3

HOW TO CRAFT A BALANCE SHEET (PART I)

How many of you can agree that it is important that we start the right way, but it's imperative that we end the right way? This continues to ring loud and clear in my conscious mind. This new decade is upon us, and it will greatly depend on our actions. How will we uphold these economic conditions we are faced with on a daily basis? Planning and preparation is the right way to start any new venture, project, and budget. Learn to implement your budget, create a balance sheet, and pay off debt. This should be the primary focus and the first order of business in your lives and households.

The overall goal is to become good stewards over the finances that you do have and to become better money managers. You want to begin saving and investing in yourself, your future, and the legacy you will leave behind on Earth. It is not only for the benefit of your family, but also for others to be able to take advantage of these opportunities. It is my hope and my prayer that you all will begin to exercise self-discipline and self-control in the area of your finances. I also hope you will be able to build your credit and a complete financial portfolio.

What is a Financial Portfolio?

A portfolio is a range of investments held by a person or organization. It is a compilation of materials that exemplifies your beliefs, skills, qualifications, education, training, and experience. It provides insight into your personality and work ethic. It is also a group of financial assets, such as stocks, bonds, commodities, currencies, and cash equivalents, as well as their fund counterparts. This includes mutual, exchanged-traded, and closed funds. Portfolios are held by investors and can be managed by financial professionals and money managers, such as yours truly.

How do we build a portfolio?

There are ten steps to building a complete financial portfolio:

1. Craft a balance sheet
2. Contribute to your 401K
3. Pay off credit card debt and installment debt
4. Open a Roth IRA
5. Purchase a home
6. Build a six-month emergency fund
7. Look into other investments
8. Invest in yourself
9. Save for your children's education (empty nesters should save for their bucket-list adventures)
10. Stay on the course

We will discuss these ten steps in my next book, Volume II of the Money Matters Mondays series, entitled *Take Ownership*. Stay tuned!

* * *

Now, let's visit a familiar passage in 1 Corinthians 4:15 (NIV).

> Even if you had ten thousand guardians in Christ, you do not have many fathers, for in Christ Jesus I became your father through the gospel.
>
> — 1 CORINTHIANS 4:15 (NIV)

Here, we take notice that Paul, who wrote the book of Corinthians, does not want the people to look at him as a leader but as a servant of God. What is a servant? A servant is a person who is a devoted, helpful follower and supporter. So, why does Paul want us to look at him as a servant? Paul wants us to realize that he is a faithful servant, follower, and supporter of God.

When we realize that we are servants of God, we are more willing to give God control of every area of our lives, even in the area of our finances. A father who loves his children unconditionally will go to the ends of this earth to provide safety and prosperity for his children. A father will sacrifice his life for the life of his children and will leave a legacy and an inheritance. When there is no time to think, a father's instinct will take over and prevent any hurt, harm, or danger to his children. The true love of a father is priceless, whether it be from our earthly father or our heavenly Father.

Know that if you receive God, the Father, He will welcome you home, no matter the situation. Just as we want a financial planner or an accountability partner to help us manage our money and investments, God wants us to manage His money and resources. He wants us to be good stewards of the many blessings He gives and provides for us.

The ability to manage money is a skill that very few of us grew up learning in school or at home. Money management is a vital skill you must acquire to reach your goals, dreams, assignments, and vision— achieving the life many desire. Asking for an accountability partner is an opportunity to learn new skills that can change the trajectory of your life and perfect the skills that you may already possess. It's also an opportunity to take possession of the gifts that have been planted inside your DNA all along. It leads you to discover your true leadership and to dominate in your area of gifting. To simplify this, one must start at the beginning – creating a budget. Start applying the new skills of being a good money manager, and be cautious and aware of your spending habits. Apply the principles and precepts to your daily lives.

Now, in order to craft a balance sheet, you must first start with a budget. What is a budget? A budget is a tool to help us manage our money. A budget shows you where your money is being spent and being received. A budget helps you to create financial stability. This budget allows you to track your expenses and follow the plan. A budget makes it easier to be responsible and accountable in paying your bills on time, building a six-month emergency fund, and saving for your next big-ticket item purchase. It is a tool needed to put an individual on a stronger financial footing for day-to-day operations and long-term goals.

Here are some examples to know where your money is being spent: housing expenses, non-housing expenses, and discretionary expenses (like entertainment, lawn care, hobbies, and sports). Here are some examples of where your money is being received: employer, self-employment, pension, social security, dividends, annuities, child support, and alimony. A budget holds you accountable. With a budget, you can begin to save for the things you need, instead of only buying the things you want. People hear the word "budget," and they cringe. Budget is not a bad word. A budget is essential for you to become a good steward of your financial matters.

An economic budget is an estimate of income and expenditure for a future period, as opposed to an account that records financial transactions.

Re-Budget: Distinguishing Wants vs. Needs

> The good person is generous and lends lavishly; no shuffling or stumbling around for this one, But a sterling and solid and lasting reputation.
>
> — PSALMS 112: 5 (MSG)

This verse deals with grace, generosity, and the use of discretion. Discretion refers to judgment and decision-making. As consumers, we must decide how a process or manner of deciding what should be done is carried out. We must decide what's proper, fitting, or right for our budget. It also means the quality of having or showing discernment or good judgment. It's the ability to make responsible decisions.

When making a budget, we must decipher our needs and wants. One must prioritize creating a budget. Start with the most important (such as needs), then move to the least important (such as wants). Here are some questions I ask myself when distinguishing wants versus needs: "Do I need this?" "Do I want this?" or "Can I afford this?"

When preparing a budget, you must include charitable donations. This is a portion of generosity and grace that is a part of your DNA. It is better to give than to receive. The majority of people understand the importance of lending to others who may need it. Alternatively, you can view generosity and grace as coming from your overflow, rather than your cup. In other words, do not lend from what is needed to sustain your own household and stability; only lend when you are carrying a surplus (additional cash-on-hand).

> But godliness with contentment is great gain. For we brought nothing into this world, and it is certain we can carry nothing out. And having food and raiment let us be therewith content. But they that will be rich fall into temptation and a snare, and into many foolish and hurtful lusts, which drown men in destruction and perdition. For the love of money is the root of all evil: which while some coveted after, they have erred from the faith, and pierced themselves through with many sorrows.
>
> — 1 TIMOTHY 6:6-10 (KJV)

Let's take a moment of truth here. If we are honest with ourselves, most of what we want isn't what we need. If you reflect even now, you have been given far more than what you actually needed. What is a need? A need is what is required (something) because it is essential or very important; expressing necessity or obligation. In order to survive, we all need food, water, clothing, shelter, and a way to earn our living. Everything outside of that is simply a want or desire. One must learn to be content, no matter what someone says or thinks of you. You should know that you are wonderfully and beautifully made – flaws and all. Your flaws are your beauty marks, which make you different and set you apart from everyone else. You and I must learn to love ourselves just the way we are— that's self-care.

I think it's time we were honest with ourselves. Our trust has been broken by individuals who have promised us things and didn't deliver. Instead of doing what they had promised or committed to, they did the exact opposite. When we put our trust, hope, and love in man, we will soon come to know the hurt, pain, and betrayal one feels when people don't keep their promise. There's only one promise keeper we can rely on: Christ Jesus, who is available 24/7. You can bank on the promises of God.

So, how do you find joy when you don't or can't get what you want? Contentment is contingent on your attitude and not your bank accounts. If you are always looking for someone else's approval, making more money, gaining more resources, and acquiring more wealth for yourself, then you are not using money how God designed it to be used. Money is a tool to provide for your needs. Money is a tool to provide for the needs of others and an opportunity to give back to God as an act of worship. By giving to God, you are declaring your satisfaction is not money but Jesus. Jesus is the one who provides for us.

Worshiping and loving money more than God can lead to pain, let downs, sin, depression, anxiety, betrayal, and deceitfulness. When we trust God to provide for our needs, we find contentment. When we trust and obey God with our money and our lives, we receive His rich love and the transformation it creates in us. A transformation lasting a lifetime ™ is a transformation to pass our legacy on as an inheritance on the earth. We are all aware that money will run out. However, God is a generous giver. He is with us throughout everything, no matter what we face— the good, the bad, and the ugly.

How to Apply Key Wisdom Principles

> Wisdom is the principal thing; therefore get wisdom: and with all thy getting get understanding.
>
> — PROVERBS 4:7 (KJV)

> Let them shout for joy, and be glad, that favor my righteous cause: yea let them say continually, Let the Lord be magnified, which hath pleasure in the prosperity of his servants.
>
> — PSALM 35:27 (KJV)

God is delighted when we, as His children, prosper. God gives us the power to get wealth, so that He may establish His covenant on the earth (Deuteronomy 8:18). God doesn't just hand it over to us. He gives us power, strength, might, and the ability to create wealth, which comes in different ways. It all starts with applying wisdom, knowledge, and understanding. Prosperity in life is to live a successful life. Wisdom is the key principle.

Using wisdom means applying what you have learned to a situation or circumstance. If you lack wisdom, you should ask God, who gives generously to all without finding fault, and it will be given to you. So, you see, wisdom can't be bought; it must be taught and received. By applying the principles and precepts, one can take full advantage of the wisdom, knowledge, and understanding of building kingdom wealth.

Prayer of Application

Father, we adore You and worship Your most Holy Name. God, we thank You for being a sovereign God— our Supreme Ruler and Ultimate Power Source.

We thank You, God, for our health and strength. We speak life, healing, and wholeness over our minds, bodies, and souls. We are healed. We are free from bondage. We are ready for the abundance and overflow You have for our lives this season. We thank You for allowing us to make sound decisions, cutting away any and everything that is not like You— cutting away those things that are hindrances in our ability to reach our goals and our vision. Help us, oh God, to set short-term and long-term goals by putting You first and asking You to bless everything we do, so our plans can succeed (Prov. 16:3, GNT).

Matthew 6:33 (GNT) says, "Instead, be concerned above everything else with the Kingdom of God and with what he requires of us, and he will provide us with all these other things." These things shall prosper us and heal us from the inside out, and our souls will prosper as well.

Help us, God, to stop procrastinating, delaying, or postponing our goals to becoming fiscally fit, financially secure, and leaving an inheritance to our children. I desire to leave my legacy in the earth. As You transform my life, transform my heart as well.

Your words say in Romans 12:2 (GNT), "Do not conform ourselves to the standards of this world, but let you, Oh God transform us inwardly by a complete change of our mind. Changing the mind-set of your people. Then we will be able to know your will God-for our lives, and what is good and is pleasing to you God and what is perfect in your sight."

> *Now the Lord is the Spirit: and where the Spirit of the Lord is there is Liberty. But we all, with open face beholding as in a glass the glory of the Lord, are changed into the same image from glory to glory, even as by the Spirit of the Lord.*
>
> — 2 CORINTHIANS 3:17–18, KJV

No more excuses. No more complaining. No more speaking death to our dreams, goals, and vision. Father, I will speak life to every situation. I will encourage myself in the Lord.

We thank you, God, that our tongue is a pen of a ready writer (Psalm 45:1). I have the ability to change the trajectory (the path) of my future with the things I speak over myself, family, marriage, and financial situations. I won't allow fear, shame, embarrassment, age, disability, or my resources to stop me from achieving financial wealth and stability.

I thank You for a sound mind, keeping me FOCUSed (Following Once Course Until Successful) on what's in front of me and not the things that are behind me. I thank You for another opportunity. Jesus tells us in Luke 9:62 (GNT) that "anyone who starts to plow and then keeps looking back is of no use for the Kingdom of God." We thank You, God, for vision and provision to keep moving forward.

We thank You that we will begin to open our mouths and speak and decree and declare Your promises over our lives and the lives of our offspring and/or household. You give us a 'yes,' and we agree with You with our 'amen.' No longer will I allow people to speak their word curses over my life or the lives of the people I love and cherish. You said, God, that whatsoever we bind on earth shall be bound in heaven, and whatsoever we loose on earth shall be loosed in heaven (Matthew 18:18 KJV). You promised us, God, that you will give us the keys of the kingdom of heaven (Matthew 16:19 KJV). God promises us that if two of us shall agree on earth as touching anything that we ask, it shall be done for us (Matthew 18:19).

Today, God, we agree with Your Word, and we are decreeing and declaring that we are living in the overflow of Your promises this season. This decade will set us up for the rest of our lives. We will follow Your precept, one precept at a time, until we have reached our divine goals, plans, and purpose that You have for us. Give us the ability to create wealth, so that you may establish Your covenant with us, the children of Abraham (Deuteronomy 8:18 KJV).

Thank you in advance, God, that you will keep us FOCUSed, committed, stable, consistent, and faithful to our divine purpose, goals, and vision. We praise and worship You for all the many blessings of overflow, abundance, and prosperity You will provide to us in this decade. I bind up the attack of any retaliatory demons that will try to come and steal this Word of knowledge. I lose Your Word, and it shall manifest in the earth through my life and the lives of my family/household. Your words shall perform the work that they were assigned to do. In Jesus's authority, we seal these prayers in the blood of Jesus.

In Jesus' mighty Authority, we pray. Amen.

* * *

4

HOW TO CRAFT A BALANCE SHEET (PART II)

Crafting a balance sheet is essential to being a good steward over your finances. It helps us understand our financial picture so that we can become healthy money managers and implement self-discipline. However, before we continue with Part 2 of this instruction, let's review the information we've discussed so far.

Recap of Part 1

Asking for an accountability partner is an opportunity to learn new skills that can change the trajectory of our lives and perfect the skills that we may already possess. The ability to manage money is a skill few of us grew up learning, but money management is vital to our success and living a happy life. Wisdom is the key principle. To make this simple, being a good money manager means being cautious and aware of our spending habits. We simply have to cut away from using decision-making and the process of making a choice. We must decide between our needs and wants. We need food, water, clothing, shelter, and an income. We want everything else. Now, in order to craft a balance sheet, we must first start a budget.

What is a budget? A budget is a tool to help us manage our money. A budget shows us where our money is being spent and where our money is being received from, like our income source(s). Here are some examples of where our money is being spent: housing expenses, non-housing expenses, and discretionary expenses. Next, the following are some examples of where our money is being received from (or our income source): employer, self-employment, pension, social security, dividends, annuities, child support, and alimony. A budget holds us accountable and can also help us to be responsible.

The budget will allow us to know what our assets or income are and what debts or liabilities we owe. The budget will also help us to see what income we have left over to be used as capital or liquid cash, which we can use to invest in ourselves or other income-generating avenues.

Debt Is A Choice

We must get free from debt. Debt is not God's best for our lives, because it prevents us from being able to do what we are called to do, for ourselves, our families, and our legacy. For example, if God called us to give extravagantly to someone in need, quit our jobs, or pack up and move to another state, could we do that right now? Are we financially prepared? Some of us may be prepared, but many of us would not be prepared for something so drastic. Whatever we are controlled by is what we are enslaved to. When we are in debt, we belong to those who we are indebted to, which are those who have lent us the money. The more debt we take on, the fewer options we give ourselves when it comes to where we work and how much we can save. Instead of making a decision based on what we want to do, we find ourselves making a decision about what we have to do. Debt will always leave us feeling stuck, confused, and helpless at times.

Retail therapy is much like it sounds. It is impulse spending or shopping to improve our mood or disposition. The world tells us we deserve nice things, regardless of whether we can afford them or not. Examples include the following: cars, new furniture, lavish vacation packages, etc. It's easy for us to get caught up in buying new things to make us feel better, and this can result in us maxing out our credit cards, while inadvertently damaging our credit scores in the process. We will deal with credit in another volume of "Money Matters Mondays." When the pressure of paying bills becomes overwhelming, we buy something new to cheer us up. It can become a vicious cycle if we don't begin exercising self-control and self-discipline in the area of our spending habits.

As followers and believers of Christ Jesus, we can be free of the burden of debt. Jesus died to free us from all forms of slavery and bondage, including credit card companies and financial lenders. Financial imprisonment is a choice. We have a choice to either give in to the temporary satisfaction of spending or to have a lasting contentment that comes from following Jesus. In Galatians 5:1 (KJV), Apostle Paul wrote: "Stand fast therefore in the liberty wherewith Christ hath made us free, and be not entangled again with the yoke of bondage." In another translation, Galatians 5:1 (MSG), it says, "Christ has set us free to live a free life. So take your stand! Never again let anyone put a harness of slavery on you." These verses of Scripture still apply to us today. God wants more for us than financial stress and a pile of bills. Jesus died for us to live in freedom, including freedom from debt.

Here are some nuggets I use before making a purchase. If a purchase costs more than $300, sleep on it. Purchase clothes out-of-season, as this offers you bigger savings. If you have a favorite store, get to know the manager. Why? The manager can apply discounts to your purchase that the cashier doesn't have the authority to apply. Make purchases based on the item's usefulness in your household. Be sure to buy quality and not quantity. Try to refrain from making purchases that don't fit your vision, plan, dreams, or assignment. Remember to set goals: set three goals a year, three goals a month, three goals a week, and three goals a day. One last nugget to apply before making a purchase is to do the following steps: wait, plan, save, invest, and use wisdom.

I hope and pray that this information is helpful to you and your household. You must begin tackling debt and saving and investing in your future. A balance sheet is much like a budget; it consists of your assets subtracted from your liabilities, which equals your capital (your income). A budget is also income subtracted from your expenses, which equals your liquid cash (your cash-on-hand or surplus).

The Life Of Freedom

One must come to the knowledge that freedom is our portion. No longer should one be bound to debt, shame, or low self-esteem because of another's opinion of them. There were often times when I was younger when I wanted people to like me and accept me into their circle. I wanted to be a part of the in-crowd, not realizing that I had more together than those I desired to be accepted by. I allowed their opinion of me to discourage me from keeping my commitment to saving and continuing to grow my financial stability. I spent my resources trying to buy their friendship and their love.

Now, little to my surprise, I accomplished neither. I walked away with less money and low self-esteem, thinking I could have done something different for them to appreciate me and the things I bought for them. Actually, when my dad went to look over my bank statements, he realized I had spent more than I usually spend. I had less on deposit than I should have in the three months of saving.

I've shared these things to encourage you to understand that it doesn't matter what others think of you. What matters is what you think of yourself. People will always have an opinion, whether negative or positive. The key takeaway is to trust your heart and follow your inner spirit.

I knew I was spending way more than I should, but I thought this would make others like me or invite me to their social events. I came to know that they didn't care about me. They only cared about how I could contribute to their bottom line.

When we allow others' opinions to outweigh our own, we need to take time to self-reflect on our own motives and intentions. Ask the hard questions. What is this benefiting me? How will I recover from the loss? Why did I allow them to use me? When will I discover my worth? When will I accept myself for who I am? When life throws us lemons, we must learn how to make lemonade.

> "Christ has set us free to live a free life. So take your stand! Never again let anyone put a harness of slavery on you…" "You were running superbly! Who cut in on you, deflecting you from the true course of obedience? This detour doesn't come from the One who called you into the race in the first place. And please don't toss this off as insignificant. It only takes a minute amount of yeast, you know, to permeate an entire loaf of bread. Deep down, the Master has given me confidence that you will not deflect. But the one who is upsetting you, whoever he is, will bear the divine judgment.
>
> — GALATIANS 5:1, 7-10 (MSG)

The Cure Comes Through Discipline

When I was a child, my parents took me to church or the Kingdom Hall, ever since I could remember. My father was chairman of the Deacon Board. My mother was a Jehovah's Witness, and my mother's mother, Mamma Dear, was an Evangelist (they have all passed on). So, I come from a line of ministers and leaders. I had to attend church every time the doors opened, whether I wanted to go or not. It was not my choice.

My parents were firm believers in raising a child in the fear of God, and that when the child becomes grown, he or she will not stray away from God. Now, I can't say I didn't stray. When I became grown, I vowed that I would never step foot in another church. I was excited that I could now make my own decisions and not be forced to attend church or the Kingdom Hall. After being alone in the world (without God and my covering), I quickly realized that I missed my church family. We were a close-knit bunch. Together, we dined, played, went shopping, went to the movies, read the Bible, and gave to help people in need in our community.

I soon discovered I was different. I was peculiar. I was not wicked. I didn't take pleasure in taking things that did not belong to me, nor did I desire to hurt people's feelings to get what I wanted. I also noticed that I did not like confrontation, arguing, and using foul language to make a point.

Once I became aware of my new surroundings, I quickly stopped hanging with that crew. I was also aware that I was becoming like them, disrespecting my elders and not listening to my inner man. After I came to this conclusion, I began going to church, studying the Bible, and socializing with people striving for the same things I longed for. I returned to the wisdom of my elders and the revelation knowledge of the Word of God.

It may look as though the grass is greener on the other side, but once you cross over, you realize there was nothing you were actually missing. You realize you have more self-discipline and self-control than those peers you were trying to impress. I realized I had a family who loved me, unconditionally. This family is the family of Believers in Christ Jesus, as well as, my own family.

It's okay to be different. It's okay to walk to the beat of a different drum. It's all right to think differently than those who were untaught or unlearned in exercising discipline, respect for self and others, and being raised in the ways of God. Embrace change. Love yourself and respect yourself for who you are and not others' opinions of you. One big lesson to learn is to forgive yourself first, then extend forgiveness to others.

> "Point your kids in the right direction– when they're old they won't be lost. The poor are always ruled over by the rich, so don't borrow and put yourself under their power. Whoever sows sin reaps weeds, and bullying anger sputters into nothing. Generous hands are blessed hands because they give bread to the poor. Kick out the troublemakers and things will quiet down; you need a break from bickering and grip-

> ing!..." "Listen carefully to wisdom; take heart what I can teach you.
>
> — PROVERBS 22:6-10, 17 (MSG)

The Responsible Citizen

To be responsible is, in short, to take accountability for your actions — being responsible for your debts, household expenses, and social activities. I can truly say, today, that I allowed things to happen in my life that did not sit well in my spirit or upbringing. I can't blame others for my own actions. I take full responsibility for budgeting my monthly income, saving, and investing in my future and the future of my children, and my children's children. I am sure to pay my taxes on time and respect my elders and leaders, even if I don't agree with them. I also take full accountability in managing my financial resources. I have learned to love even those who have lied to me, treated me with disrespect, and those who have hurt me physically and mentally.

Yes, I know you may be saying, "I would make sure that those who hurt me see the hurt I put back on them." However, I choose to allow Father God to bring His justice and wrath. This way, I have no guilt in my conscience and can sleep well at night. God sees all and knows all. There is nothing He does not know. I live in this reality, as I have seen God fight my battles and give me victory over my circumstances— *clean victory!*

> That's also why you pay taxes— so that an orderly way of life can be maintained. Fulfill your obligations as a citizen. Pay your taxes, pay your bills, respect your leaders. Don't run up debts, except for the huge debt of love you owe each other. When you love others, you complete what the law has been after all along.
>
> — ROMANS 13:6-8 (MSG)

Prayer of Encouragement

Jesus, I thank You for giving me the ability to live free from debt, and I thank You for my freedom. Help me, as I serve You alone, putting You in charge of my plans, dreams, goals, assignments, and my income source.

Lord, give me the courage to live in freedom, instead of returning to my old ways. Help me to stop procrastinating, complaining, and making excuses for my financial stability.

My God, You are the only One who can fulfill the longings of my heart for a life free of stress, debt, or any bondages that hold me back from what Your Word promises me. Your Word promises me dominion, authority, power, love, and a sound mind. You have given me dominion and power. God, help me realize how powerful I am and that I can do all things through Christ that strengthens me.

In Jesus' mighty Name, we pray. Amen.

* * *

House Fund

5

LEARNING TO INVEST IN YOUR FUTURE

Investments and savings are important, because in today's world, just earning money is not enough. We work hard for the money we earn. But when it's time to retire, do we have adequate funds to lead a comfortable lifestyle or fulfill our dreams and goals? We must invest our money wisely and get a return on our investments. Is there a risk involved? Of course, with any investment or savings avenue, you must weigh the costs and benefits.

Understanding Investment Terms & Concepts

What is an investment? An investment is an action or process of investing money for profit or material results. Investment (or investing) means that an asset is bought, or that money is put into a bank to get future interest from it. Investment is also the total amount of money spent by a shareholder buying shares of a company.

What is a shareholder? A shareholder is an owner of a company as determined by the number of shares they own. A shareholder can be an individual or a corporate entity (commonly known as a corporate shareholder) who owns a share or multiple shares of the company. In economic management sciences, investments mean long-term savings.

Why is investing important? Investing ensures present and future long-term financial security. The money generated from your investments can provide financial security and income. The following are several ways to invest: stocks, bonds, and ETFs (Exchange Traded Funds). This provides us income in the form of a dividend.

What is a dividend? A dividend is a payment made by a corporation to its shareholders, usually as a distribution of profits (income). Each shareholder receives a dividend based on how many shares they own. Dividends are allocated as fixed amounts per share. Dividends can provide us with a steady stream of income.

Your Attitude Towards Investing

Consider the following story from the Book of Matthew.

> "It's also like a man going off on an extended trip. He called his servants together and delegated responsibilities. To one he gave five thousand dollars, to another two thousand, to a third one thousand, depending on their abilities. Then he left. Right off, the first servant went to work and doubled his master's investment. The second did the same. But the man with the single thousand dug a hole and carefully buried his master's money.
>
> After a long absence, the master of those three servants came back and settled up with them. The one given five thousand dollars showed him how he had doubled his investment. His master commended him: 'Good Work! You did your job well. From now on, be my partner.' The servant with the two thousand showed how he also had doubled his master's investment. His master commended him: 'Good Work! You did your job well. From now on, be my partner.' The

> servant given one thousand said, 'Master, I know you have high standards and hate careless ways, that you demand the best and make no allowances for error. I was afraid I might disappoint you, so I found a good hiding place and secured your money. Here it is, safe and sound down to the last cent.' The master was furious.
>
> 'That's a terrible way to live! It's criminal to live cautiously like that! If you knew I was after the best, why did you do less than the least? The least you could have done would have been to invest the sum with the bankers, where at least I would have gotten a little interest. Take the thousand and give it to the one who risked the most. And get rid of this "play-it-safe" who won't go out on a limb. Throw him out into utter darkness.'
>
> — MATTHEW 25:14-30 (MSG)

In most Bibles, the words from Jesus are denoted in red lettering. In this passage, Jesus is speaking to us. He is giving us a parable to live by and giving us instructions on how to invest and save in our future. This was the first business and leadership conference held that is known to mankind. Jesus is telling us that we are to first be responsible in our daily lives, and when we have multiple things on our plates, we must learn to delegate.

What is delegation? To delegate means entrusting a person with a task or responsibility; it can also mean authorizing a person to represent others, which can be a member of a committee. Jesus was giving the servants authority to bring back the most return for the money they had to invest. Every great leader knows how, when, and what to delegate authority to their people. Jesus made no mistake in delegating the authority; He knew the end result before He gave the servants the money to invest. The strongest servant was given five thousand dollars to invest; the next servant was given two thousand dollars; and the least of the servants was given one thousand dollars. It says in the Scripture that the money was given to them according to their abilities.

I surmise that the servant with the five thousand dollars must have maintained a well-run household. I say this because he knew exactly what to do to get the biggest return on his investments, meaning he must have done his homework. As a result, he could move quickly and get the best results. Now, with the second servant, I surmise he went to the first servant for wise counsel, and he followed the careful instructions given to him to receive the same outcome as the first servant, having 100% return on his investments.

As a lesson, we must move quickly and expediently when we get a hot lead or find out about a good return on the investment avenue. Share the information, so that others can take advantage of the same benefits and receive a larger return on their investments. Who doesn't want a 100% return on their investments? Don't let fear and doubt take over your thoughts and actions, because this can cause you to miss out on God's blessings and abundance for you and your household.

We all desire to hear Jesus say, "Well done, thy good and faithful servant. You have been faithful over a few things. I will make thee ruler over many things; enter thou into the joy of thy Lord" (Matthew 25:23). Jesus was so pleased with the first two servants' actions that He invited them to be His partner.

We all want to be in a good partnership, and we desire our partners to have similar characteristics as ourselves. In a partnership, two or more people agree to position themselves as business partners in a company or firm with shared financial responsibility. What is characteristic? According to the Oxford English Dictionary, a characteristic is "a feature or quality belonging typically to a person, place, or thing and serving to identify it." We want to surround ourselves with like-minded people who help us to grow. It is important to have people who will challenge our thought processes and hold us accountable for our actions and words. We also need people who are not afraid of taking risks and who sow seeds. A seed must die to become a beautiful plant or vegetable for harvest time.

The third servant went about his investment with fear and trembling. Thus, he dug a hole in the ground and placed the money there for safekeeping. He was probably afraid that he would spend the money his master had given him, or he was just too lazy to do his research to find the best use of his money. Maybe he was too afraid to ask for help. We can all sympathize with the third servant. Sometimes we have been uncertain, not knowing the outcome, and too afraid or embarrassed to ask for help.

Growing up, I was taught that any question not asked is more than likely the question everyone wants to know the answer to, but is too embarrassed to ask. Therefore, we must learn to ask as many questions as necessary. Any question not asked is a question we will never get answered by the very people who can help us increase our knowledge and understanding.

So, the third servant wanted to play it safe due to his fear, slothfulness, inability to seek wise counsel, and possible negative influence from others. Matthew 25: 26-27 (MSG) says, "The master was furious. 'That's a terrible way to live! It's criminal to live cautiously like that! If you knew I was after the best, why did you do less than the least? The least you could have done would have been to invest the sum with the bankers, where at least I would have gotten a little interest.'" Fear can cripple our advancement and hinder our success.

The Lord encourages us to save and invest our money or, at the very least, to take advantage of some interest or return on our investments. He could have put the money in a savings account, a money market, a Certificate of Deposit (CD), an Individual Retirement Account (IRA), or an annuity. Proverbs 18:9 (GW) says, "Whoever is lazy in his work is related to a vandal." We do not want to be thrown out into utter darkness because of fear, laziness, or just plain ignorance. We have the ability and the resources to inquire and receive detailed information on several savings and investment avenues. We must learn to research our interests before jumping in head first. We must lay out every possible savings or investment avenue, side-by-side, and weigh the costs, risks, and benefits. This is the reasonable service we owe to ourselves and our household. We must exercise wisdom, self-discipline, and self-control to leave an inheritance to the next generation.

We are the lenders and not borrowers. We are the head and not the tail. We are victorious and overcomers. We are God's very own masterpiece; God created us in His image and likeness, to be creative. God causes us to gain wealth. Second Timothy 1:7-8 (GW) says, "For the Spirit God gave us does not make us timid, but gives us power, love, and self-discipline. So do not be ashamed of the testimony about our Lord or of me, His prisoner. Rather, join with me in suffering for the gospel, by the power of God. God didn't give us a cowardly spirit but a spirit of power, love, and good judgment."

When situations arise that we are unsure of or have no knowledge of, it's time for us to go to work, not feeling intimidated or defeated because of our uncertainty or lack of knowledge. It's time to roll up our sleeves and dive in. Ask questions to get clarity, and ask for help. Remember, knowledge is power. God has given us wisdom, knowledge, and understanding. God desires us to prosper in all of our dealings in life. Keep seeking until all secrets are revealed. Ask God for His revelation knowledge and a clear sign to move forward.

Let's look at it this way. God is the supplier of everything on Earth and in Heaven above. Step out of fear, and exercise your faith. Walk in victory over every situation, curveball, disappointment, and health challenge; know that our God is with us. God causes us to prosper! Take a leap of faith, and watch God do just what you asked of Him. He may not come through when you want Him, but I am a living eyewitness that God is always on time. Stop procrastinating, and begin investing in your future, dreams, and goals.

God desires for us to be wealthy, healthy, and wise citizens of His Kingdom and of the Covenant's promises. We do not need to be concerned with what the next person has. Instead, we should focus on what we have and how we manage what God has given us. Be careful of coveting another person's blessing, because you don't know what they had to go through to receive the blessing and favor of God. God doesn't make mistakes like giving you my blessings;

God knows just what He is doing. His Word tells us that He gives to us according to our abilities and our faith.

Fellow Believers, let's get busy doing our homework, research, and investing to save for our future. Let's be prosperous, generous givers, and wise investors that are ready to walk into our wealthy place God has already prepared for us since the beginning. It all starts with budgeting. So, make a commitment today to start your household budget with your immediate family and children. Start the children young, so that when they grow older, they will return to the knowledge, understanding, and wisdom being taught at home.

Prayer of Faith

Father God, we thank You for blessing us according to our ability and faith. Increase our abilities and increase our faith. Create in us a clean heart, O Lord — a heart after your very own heart. Thank You, God, for giving us wisdom, knowledge, and understanding. Thank You, God, for good health and a sound mind.

Having wisdom is knowing that if we acknowledge God and seek wise counsel first in all we do, then we will be successful. Help us to meditate on Your Word and apply Your words to our lives, daily. Help me to ask for help when I don't fully understand. Help me to weigh the cost of my investments and savings vehicles, to inspect what I expect. Help me to be creative in my thinking. Help us to be wealthy in our homes, financial matters, investments, relationships, health, and communities. God help me to be enthusiastic about my future and my family's future, saving and investing money on a weekly or monthly basis, and creating a legacy for my family's inheritance.

We decree and declare that we will line up with Your Word and Your Will for our lives.

In Jesus' mighty Authority, we pray. Amen.

* * *

6

WHAT ARE YOUR INVESTMENTS?

What is a resource? According to the Oxford English Dictionary, a resource is "a stock or supply of money, materials, staff, and other assets that can be drawn on by a person or organization to function, effectively." The Oxford English Dictionary also defines it as "an action or strategy which may be adopted in adverse circumstances."

Stewarding Your Resources

This is a good time to reflect on how you use the resources that are made available to you and your household. Take inventory of your possessions, and allocate the findings to those who are in need of assistance. Because our future generations are watching us closely, our future depends on how we invest today. We must set an example of how to invest properly. First, start at home, and then give from your overflow of resources. It is essential to start at home and invest in yourself first. Don't forget to reward yourself for the hard work, talent, and treasure you've put into your job. You should start by investing at least 10% back into your future and the legacy you want to leave on the earth. Here are some questions to ponder over when allocating the findings of your resources: Are you giving generously to those less fortunate than you? Are you helping the orphans or the widows? Are you helping the homeless? Are you feeding the poor? Are you helping to clothe those that are without clothing? Are you helping to advance the kingdom? What are you doing with your resources? The goal is to start our children young, teaching them to be cheerful givers. We must teach our children to invest in themselves first, then give to those who could use a helping hand. When we do these things, we can expect our overflow to continue flowing. In order to receive, you must release. By releasing, you make room for more.

> "Do not store up riches for yourselves here on earth, where moths and rust destroy, and robbers break in and steal. Instead, store up riches for yourselves in heaven, where moths and rust cannot destroy, and robbers cannot break in and steal. For your heart will always be where your riches are. The eyes are like a lamp for the body. If your eyes are sound, your whole body will be full of light; but if your eyes are no good, your body will be in darkness. So if the light in you is darkness, how terribly dark it will be! No one can be a slave of two masters; he will hate one and love the other; he will be loyal to one and despise the other. You cannot serve both God and money."
>
> — MATTHEW 6:19-24 (GNB)

There are some specific things Jesus wants you to pay attention to. Your heart is where your treasure is. Therefore, it is time for a heart check. Are you investing your resources in the world's management system, or are you investing in God's management system? The world's management system would have you investing in the latest designer clothes, the newest technology, the newest car, and this season's hot buys for children and adults. Matthew 6:33 says, "But seek ye first the kingdom of God, and his righteousness; and all these things will be added unto you" (KJV). There is no need to chase after things that add no value to your wildest dreams, visions, goals, and assignments.

We must understand that our trash is someone else's treasure. Be mindful of others who are less fortunate than you when cleaning and preparing for the next season. The rule of thumb is that if you have not worn or used it in the past two years, it can be given away. Those old clothes can be given to someone who has no nice clothes. Those gym shoes or boots you no longer desire to wear can be given to someone with no shoes. Those coats, sweaters, or jackets that you have not worn can be given to someone who doesn't have the resources to purchase one. Those canned goods that you have in your cabinets that you are overlooking can feed people with nothing to eat. The furniture you are replacing can be given to a shelter that houses people with nothing to restart their lives.

You have more resources than you realize. We can give to others from our overflow or just by thinking of others more than we think of ourselves. Seasons change, and in every season, you can give, share, care, and show love and kindness to one another. We should be doing this all year long— giving back to our community and showing our children that giving is better than receiving.

When you release your overflow, your household will continually be shocked by your needs, wants, and desires. The secret is to give and sow seeds, so that you may receive your harvest. Are we purchasing gifts for others to receive a gift in return, or are we purchasing gifts to show our love and appreciation? Our lives should reflect the person we are on the inside. Our hearts should be outwardly reflecting our inner man. We should keep watch over the things we see, by keeping our eyes focused on the important things. We also must send up our treasure in heaven and not here on this earth. For earthly things will pass away, and only what you do for God will last throughout all eternity.

Are you focusing your eyes on the things you are receiving? If you are focusing on the things you can get, then your eyes are filled with the darkness of this world and not the light of Christ. You are not seeing clearly, and these things could be leading you astray from the abundance and overflow awaiting you and your household. Protecting your eye gates is just as important as protecting what you hear and what you speak to one another.

We are to encourage ourselves and others instead of judging one another. We are to love one another and show genuine concern for others and their needs. Forgive quickly, and love God. You can not love both God and money – it's either one or the other. We cannot have it both ways. Giving is a requirement of the free will you and I have been given. The more you and I give, the more our focus is on God and the love He has for us and our fellow man. The more you stay closed-fisted, the more selfish and self-centered you become. In 2 Corinthians 9:7 (KJV), it says, "Every man according as he purposely in his heart, so let him give; not grudgingly, or of necessity: for God loveth a cheerful giver." Giving is a mirror to your soul and your heart. Let us take inventory of our motives and actions.

What is the reflection of your heart today? Know there will be times when your faith will be stretched. Are you aware that our physical bodies need to stretch daily? We have to stretch our muscles and bodies to stay healthy and flexible. The mind, the heart, and the spirit man also need to be stretched. We stunt our growth when we fail to stretch in these vital areas of our lives. Are you aware that everyone must undergo a testing process to grow?

I challenge you, today, to begin to look forward to a God-inspired life and stretch your faith. Believe that God will provide the very things that you are asking for. Believe in your future and that God has a wealthy place for you. Believe that you are the head and not the tail. Believe that you are victorious in all your life endeavors. Believe that you are the lender and not the borrower. Ask God for broader horizons and greater victories.

The God we serve is huge; yes, you and I are part of His big plan. We need to ask for bigger blessings, faith, and imagination. God says that if you can think it, you can receive it, and by faith, you can achieve it. Embrace the new applications. Go through the process of being stretched, developed, and matured today. Rest in knowing and believing that God can and is able to do exceedingly, abundantly, and above all you could ever ask, think, or imagine.

Watch the company that you keep. Leave all negativity and dream-demolishers behind, as these types of personalities will crush your dreams and leave you feeling empty and hopeless. Learn to keep company with wise counsel. Surround yourself with people who can help you and advise you on how to achieve the goals, dreams, visions, and assignments you have set for yourself and the legacy you want to leave on this earth. Wise counsel can be a mentor, an accountability partner, or someone who has a proven track record on budgeting, savings, and investments. A financial planner or consultant, like myself, helps you to acquire your life-long dreams, visions, goals, and assignments.

Preparing a Budget

The time to start budgeting is now. Begin a weekly, bi-monthly, or monthly regimen to invest in self-care. Invest 10% in your future and another 10% in charitable donations. This is the way to financial freedom, and one must start at the beginning. It takes practice, consistency, commitment, discipline, and self-control to become successful.

There comes a time in one's life when one needs to put shame and embarrassment behind them. At one point or time in our lives, we all have made mistakes and have made a mess of our finances. It is time to walk into the assurance of guidance. Proverbs 3:5-6 says, "Trust in the Lord with all thine heart; and lean not unto thine own understanding. In all thy ways acknowledge him, and he shall direct thy paths" (KJV). God allows us to create wealth and riches; He instructs us to invest in ourselves and the commonwealth of God's kingdom.

Today, I encourage you to commit these Scripture verses to memory and meditate on them daily. Deuteronomy 8:18 says, "Remember that it is the Lord your God who gives you the power to become rich. He does this because he is still faithful today to the covenant that he made with your ancestors" (GNB). The King James Version of this verse says, "But thou shalt remember the Lord thy God: for it is he that giveth thee power to get wealth, that he may establish his covenant which he sware unto thy fathers, as it is this day."

The book of Proverbs is a book of wisdom. Proverbs 4:7 says, "Wisdom is the principal thing; therefore get wisdom: and with all thy getting get understanding" (KJV). God reminds us all throughout the Scripture about wisdom, knowledge, and understanding. Exodus 31:3 says, "And I have filled him with the spirit of God, in wisdom, and in understanding, and in knowledge, and in all manner of workmanship" (KJV).

Make a budget, and stick to the plan, as much as possible. When you first start, use a pencil. because you will need to make some adjustments through the planning stages. If you notice you are coming up in the red (negative), erase it and make some minor or major adjustments and corrections. If you are consistently in the negative, do not give up, and keep allocating your funds to pay down debt. Eventually, you will look up and see you have paid the deficit off and are now working in the black (surplus), which is a positive direction when preparing a budget.

Income Reflection: A Transformation That Lasts a Lifetime ™

As you learn to invest in yourself and the commonwealth of the kingdom, I would like to leave you with something I have used over the years to help me become financially stable, credit-worthy, and debt free. To help you make better use of your money, here are a few ways to divide your finances:

- Invest 50% of your money in your checking account. This is a way to ensure that you have enough money to pay your mortgage/rent, car payment, student loans, utilities, food, and other miscellaneous bills.

- Invest 15% of your money on tithes and offerings. If you have no church home, you can give 15% to a local ministry or a local church in your community; you can also make a charitable donation.

- Invest 10% of your money into entertainment, shopping, dining out, and other desires.

- Invest 10% of your money into long-term investments (such as ROTH IRA, 401K, mutual funds, real estate, or money that you reinvest and never spend).

- Invest 15% of your money into short-term savings (such as money markets, Certificate of Deposits, emergency funds, car repairs, house repairs, or large purchases).

This strategy is durable and will prepare you for financial stability. It teaches you discipline, structure, responsibility, and the ability to live within your means. As you pay off debt and receive additional income (like a raise at work, profit-sharing, bonuses, etc.), you could increase your percentages to savings and investment vehicles. Learning to invest in yourself and in others are key principles to financial growth, creditworthiness, financial literacy, and creating wealth. You must start somewhere. So, why not start today?

The first key factor in creating and maintaining a budget is analyzing your credit report and building a stable portfolio. We must all learn to be good stewards of our financial matters. The money that God has entrusted into your hands is very important. How you manage the money will tell how well you are able to manage your financial resources.

The second key factor in creating and maintaining a budget is knowing where your money is going. In the current, there is constant movement. Just like a current, money is active, which is why it is called currency. To the natural eye, one can misjudge a current flow. While a current of water may appear like it is not moving, it is actually moving rather quickly as one can quickly be overtaken by its rapid movement. It's important to know the flow of your currency. One day you can have plenty of money (surplus), and the next day, it could be gone. You must take control of your finances, by first creating a budget. As discussed in the previous chapters, the biggest part of managing your money is knowing where your money is and how much you have available (which is liquid cash-on-hand).

Proverbs 27:23 says, "Be thou diligent to know the state of thy flocks, and look well to thy herds" (KJV). What does this mean? I am glad you asked. It is broken down in plain, old layman's terms, which means "to look well to our responsibilities" and "be accountable for our own actions and circumstances." In Biblical times, flocks and herds were used as currency. That's how the people measured their wealth and left a family inheritance. When building wealth, they knew everything about how many flocks and herds they had. It's no different compared to today's society. If we desire to have financial wealth or experience financial freedom, you and I must learn to manage our money well. Learn to inspect what we expect; that means start that budget on paper, on purpose, and at the beginning of every month. With new technology, you can find an app to assist with preparing your budget and paying your debt.

The third key factor of the art of budgeting is building up your emergency funds; this is to have three to six months' worth of reserves, in case of an unforeseen emergency. We live in post-pandemic times, where many people are not prepared with reserves or emergency funds. Here's a moment of truth. I would have been struggling to stay above water if I had not had the six months of reserves in place. Although I work and have income, I could have been climbing out of a deficit myself without properly managing my resources. It pays to save, plan, and invest. You have to save and invest now for your future. You will soon look around and see the future staring you in the face, and you won't be prepared. This is why planning is essential, and short-term and long-term goals are a must.

Today, I'm encouraging you to start preparing for your future. If you sit around thinking: "I will get to it," then soon, you will notice that a lack of management of your finances will leave you with very few resources. This will affect your ability to live a comfortable peaceful life in the present and future. Anything worth having is worth sacrificing for. Evaluate your finances; plan for purchases; and save for the things you want. Planning ahead is the secret to your success and financial stability. Tell your money who is the boss, and create those budgets with a pencil, paper, and calculator in hand. Make your money work for you, instead of you working for the money.

Prayer of Increased Faith and Grace

> Keep company with the wise and you will become wise. If you make friends with stupid people, you will be ruined.
>
> — PROVERBS 13:20 GNB

Father God, we come giving thanks. Thank You, God, for always being there when we need You. Thank You, God, that You take care of every one of our needs. Thank You, God, that in our weakness, You make us strong. Thank You, God, that You know our hearts, and Your Word promises to give us our hearts' desires. Thank You, God, that You are our master, and we serve You and only You. Thank You, God, for our health and strength. Thank You, God, that Your grace and mercy show up brand new every day. Every day, You are the same. You don't change.

God, if I or anyone in my household have done anything to sin against Thee, please forgive us of all our sins. If our sins were committed by omission or commission, we now ask for forgiveness and repent of any sins. Forgive us, God, for not trusting You in every area of our lives.
Increase our faith. Help us in our unbelief. Help us to step out of our comfort zones and our familiar areas. Help us to trust You, even when we can't trace You. Help us to depend solely on You. Your Word clearly tells us not to worry.

Matthew 6:25–27, 34 says, "This is why I tell you not to be worried about the food and drink you need in order to stay alive, or about clothes for your body. After all. Isn't life worth more than food? And isn't the body worth more than clothes? Look at the birds: they do not sow seeds, gather a harvest and put it in barns; yet our Father in heaven takes care of them! Aren't you worth much more than birds? Can any of you live a bit longer by worrying about it? So do not worry about tomorrow; it will have enough worries of its own. There is no need to add to the troubles each day brings" (GNB).

Worrying and being stressed out show us how much faith we have to believe and trust in Your Word. Help us, God, to deepen our faith, trust, and belief in your Word, knowing that Your words are truth. We know Your words cannot come back void, and they must perform the work they set out to do.

God, we invite Your Holy Spirit to come in and sup with us in our homes, jobs, and everywhere we go. Holy Spirit, lead and guide us into all truth. Let not our hearts be troubled about the things of the world. Instead, God, You lift up our hearts, our minds, and our thoughts to "whatsoever things are true, whatsoever things are honest, whatsoever things are just, whatsoever things are pure, whatsoever things are lovely, whatsoever things are of good report; if there be any virtue and if there be any praise, think on these things" (Philippians 4:8 KJV). For, God, we desire to live our lives pleasing unto You for this is our reasonable service (Romans 12:1 KJV).

Increase our wisdom. Increase our knowledge. Increase our understanding. Increase our discernment. Increase us "with good will doing service, as to the Lord, and not to men (Ephesians 6:7 KJV). Help us take a long look at nature today and realize that if You can take care of the birds in the air, fish in the sea, wildlife, and the trees, surely you can take care of Your prized possession, which is us, Your children.

You have made us and not us ourselves. Increase us, God, in every area You choose today. For You, oh God, know just what we need before we even ask. Supply our needs according to your riches in glory. Give us overflow and abundance. To whom much is given also much is required. Give us strength where we are weak. Give us the ability to create wealth and riches. Give us the ability to step out of our comfort zones and launch into deep territories, as you move us into our next purpose— our assignments on the earth. Keep us strong, steadfast, and immovable, always working to advance the Kingdom of God right here on earth. Matthew 6:33 says, "But seek ye first the kingdom of God, and his righteousness; and all these things will be added unto you" (KJV).

In Jesus' authority, I ask these prayers and seal them in Jesus' blood. I bind up any attack on these prayers of retaliation, trying to steal the spoken word over our lives. God, we ask that You fulfill these prayers and the unspoken prayers of our hearts.

In Jesus' mighty Name, we pray. Amen.

* * *

STATES OF AMERICA
THE UNITED STATES OF AMERICA
MB 09905306 A

7

SUPPLY AND DEMAND

As a reminder, it is God who supplies us with our needs. Our basic needs are food, water, shelter, clothing, and financial resources (or income).

> "But my God shall supply all your need according to his riches in glory by Christ Jesus."
>
> — PHILIPPIANS 4:19 (KJV)

In the face of today's challenges, such as the COVID-19 pandemic, God is the one who provides for us. When the pandemic first began, many of us were worried, asking questions like: "How are we going to pay our bills, keep a roof over our heads, and have food on the table?" It has been three years and several months since the world was shut down, having limited resources available.

God's power, strength, and faithfulness have been demonstrated throughout this difficult time. Many of us have received stimulus checks and governmental assistance on top of our bi-weekly unemployment stipend. SNAP benefits have been extended to assist in keeping needy families fed. Social security and disability recipients have also received the "stimulus package." The state legislators have allowed people to apply for benefits as long as they have a physical address. In contrast to the past, self-employed workers (like Uber, Lyft, and construction workers) are now eligible for benefits. If you are a citizen of the United States of America and have not received this benefit (due to unemployment), please see a tax preparer to file your 1040 form for the years 2020, 2021, and 2022. These benefits are available to every American citizen, regardless if you had employment or were unemployed. *(Note: The only way the IRS can send your benefits to you is by filing your 1040 form for the years listed above.)*

God is your source who provides all of your resources. While your money may run out, God is a generous giver, and He has the unlimited ability to make ways out of no ways for you and your household. No matter what you face– good, bad, or indifferent– God is with you to see you through everything, despite what the world may say.

> "For I am the Lord your God who takes hold of your right hand and says to you, Do not Fear; I will help you."
>
> — ISAIAH 41:13 (NIV)

It is time for every believer to renew their faith in God. Repent of your sins and rebellion and return to God's unmerited grace. Yes, there have been some casualties of this spiritual warfare, and there are still less fortunate people than you and I.

> "Let's take a good look at the way we're living and reorder our lives under God. Let's lift our hearts and hands at one and the same time, praying to God in heaven: We've been contrary and willful, and you haven't forgiven."
>
> — LAMENTATIONS 3:40-42 (MSG)

Thus, it is our responsibility to help those and give cheerfully our time, talents, and treasure to those who are in need. We must trust God to provide for our needs. You can find contentment in God and make a demand on the Word of God!

Find Contentment and Joy

Contentment is contingent on your attitude and perception, not your bank accounts. If you always strive for more money, resources, and wealth for yourself, then you are not using money how God designed it to be used. Money is a tool to provide for our needs, the needs of others, and an opportunity to give back to God as an act of worship. By giving to God, you declare your satisfaction is Jesus, not money. Planning and using wisdom are the keys for your success.

> "And the LORD answered me, and said, Write the vision, and make it plain upon tables, that he may run that readeth it."
>
> — HABAKKUK 2:2 (KJV)

> "Let them shout for joy, and be glad, that favour my righteous cause: yea, let them say continually, Let the Lord be magnified, which hath pleasure in the prosperity of his servants."
>
> — PSALMS 35:27 (KJV)

God finds delight when you, as His child, prospers. It is your inheritance to live debt free, healthy, wealthy, rich, and wise.

> "But thou shalt remember the LORD thy God: for it is he that giveth thee power to get wealth, that he may establish his covenant which he sware unto thy fathers, as it is this day."

— DEUTERONOMY 8:18 (KJV)

God doesn't just give us wealth and prosperity. He gives us power, strength, might, and the ability to attain wealth, which comes in many forms, but all start with wisdom. Prosperity in life is a successful life. What does it mean to be prosperous? According to the Oxford English Dictionary, it means "to be successful in material terms and flourishing financially." You have the ability to live a prosperous life in every area of your life. The real question is, do you believe this? If you believe, it is time to put a demand on the unlimited supply that is in-store for you and your household.

> "For God hath not given us the spirit of fear; but of power, and of love, and of a sound mind."
>
> — 2 TIMOTHY 1:7 (KJV)

Be encouraged today, and do not allow fear to demobilize you from aggressively pursuing your dreams, visions, goals, and assignments. You are set apart, a royal priesthood, and a chosen people; therefore, you are not to be a partaker in this world's systems and tactics. Come boldly, and put a demand on the Word of God. Be confident in knowing that these passages of Scripture I have shared with you will keep you uplifted and focused on becoming who you are designed to be. The acronym for F.O.C.U.S. stands for: Follow One Course Until Success.

God is bringing balance, order, harmony, and unity back to the family unit. Communication is one of the keys to any successful relationship. Listening with empathy and paraphrasing what you have heard is important. This lets your family member know you have heard the concerns or requests with clarity. This also helps to disarm or dismantle misunderstanding, pride, disagreements, and undeserving treatment. The underlying issues in any relationship must be addressed for harmony, unity, balance, and order to be restored.

During pre-pandemic times, we lived in a busy world of multitasking that left many underlying issues unnoticed; but when the pandemic began, pre-existing relationship problems were brought to light. Now, the opportunity has presented itself to take advantage of repairing the relationship with a spouse, family member, friend, or co-worker. Now is the time to hear, listen, correct, and apologize for past behavior or actions. Family is essential to God's plan for you and me to prosper in unity, love, forgiveness, and right living.

Forgiveness requires us to surrender ourselves, our pride, and the right to be offended. However, this is exactly what Christ implores us to do, which is to love each other as we love ourselves; to receive forgiveness whilst offering forgiveness without an apology; and to extend grace without any condition. It is a challenge to be able to rise to a higher standard. Forgiveness is not a fleshly activity; it is spiritual, but we often forgive, expecting a fleshly response. We even often become disheartened because the act of forgiving someone has not appeased our flesh.

As Believers, one of the core elements of the relationship with God is forgiveness. There are often times when one feels compelled to be angry, seek vengeance, or desire to cause bodily harm to another. These are all fleshly reactions. I know we all make mistakes and have shortcomings as we all have fallen short of the glory of God. I know there have been times in my life when I failed God miserably because I was hurt, broken, and confused. I thought life couldn't get any worse as my immediate family appeared to be in shambles. I was heartbroken and felt lost and alone. God takes our mistakes and shortcomings and turns them around for our good. He takes our mess and makes it His masterpiece to get glory out of our lives. This season that we are in is no different.

God works all things together for our good. No! It does not look good; nor does it feel good as the pain and stress can become overwhelming. But God gave us Jesus, and through Jesus, there is resurrection. Jesus left us the Holy Spirit, our Divine Comforter, Guide, and Abba Father (meaning "source"). Through it all, I realized that Abba Father is my source and controls all the resources. I learned to let go and let God handle my fear, insecurities, hurt, and pain.

Gaining clarity of mind is the beginning of prosperity and success in our planning.

Living in Goshen

Goshen was a place of comfort and plenty. According to Genesis 45:10, the King of Egypt gave this land to Jacob and his descendants. They lived there until the Exodus. This passage of Scripture demonstrates an important life lesson. Money can't buy your protection, peace, agape love, or joy. We must partner with God for that. A partner is when two people agree and engage in the same activity.

When I decided to partner with God, my life took a pivotal turn. During the lockdown, many either decided not to go to the house of worship or could not go because their house of worship was closed. It was a time when we all realized that a building made of brick and mortar is not where God is. God is in the hearts, minds, bodies, and souls of every Believer. In your home, prepare an altar for God and a quiet place where you can spend time, reading, meditating, talking, and listening to God and the subconscious mind. God is ready to take you to the next level. The next level comes with going through a process of challenges and situations— overcoming them all with victory.

Let's go back to Genesis 12:7. It says, "And the Lord appeared unto Abram, and said, Unto thy seed will I give this land: and there builded he an altar unto the Lord, who appeared unto him" (KJV). God delivers your supply each and every day, and this is a promise of God. As you start out this new life or new decade, you can come into agreement and partner with God. Stand on the promises of God with your focus on budgeting, preparing balance sheets, and building a complete financial portfolio. You must stay F.O.C.U.S.ed, following one course until successful. God is ready to add His "super" to our "natural" and provide us with supernatural blessings of overflow, abundance, prosperity, wealth, health, and healing.

Believe in God for debt cancellations. Believe in God to have excellent credit and FICO score. Believe in God for savings and investments. Believe in Him for healing, good health, and deliverance. Believe in God for your new home and new job. Whatever you are believing God for, believe, and do not doubt. Watch God bring it to pass.

Ask God to increase your wisdom, knowledge, and understanding of how to apply these principles and precepts to your lives. The world may be in a recession, but it is time for every believer to take possession. Take it by force, if necessary. God gives you the ability to create wealth. So, spend time developing your prayer life and meditation time, daily. I am a living witness that through prayer and meditation, God will give you new, witty ideas, solutions to problems, and peace, like a still river.

This is your opportunity to get your relationships, mindset, and finances in order. Do this while learning to distinguish between your wants and needs. Your needs should be food, water, shelter, clothing, and financial resources. Everything else is a want. It is essential to save money and budget. You must know where your money is going. You must break the bad habits of spending and exercise self-discipline and self-control. According to the Oxford English Dictionary, spending means to "pay out, disburse, or expend"; it also means "to dispose of money, wealth, resources, etc. without proper planning."

Decrees and Declarations

Help me, Father God, to be prepared and ready to change my mindset. Change my thought patterns to align with Your Word. Transform my heart, so that my life will reflect a transformation lasting a lifetime™. Instill in me courage to share the truth of the Gospel with my family, loved ones, friends, and foes alike, as the Bible has much to say regarding managing finances and debt. Help me God to take ownership of the covenant promises You made with my ancestors, Abraham, Issac, and Jacob. Help me to be accountable for my actions. Help me to stop playing the blame game, complaining, and bickering. Let us (me and my household) Worship You, Father, in Spirit and in Truth. I decree and declare clarity of thought, mind, soul, and spirit.

Help me Father, to realize that I am the Church, and a part of the Body of Christ. The very gates of hell cannot stand against me nor my household. If

God be for us, then who can stand against us (Romans 8:31)? Whom shall we fear (Psalm 27:1)? Victory is ours. Peace is ours. We must plan and prepare for victorious living.

Commit to Him today, and give God your best and first. Surrender it all to God. Put God first in every situation or decision, because He is the game changer. He has been preparing us for such a time as this. Put on the full armor of God, as it is our battle gear of protection from the fiery darts of the enemy's attacks in this spiritual war. Stand strong, stay consistent, and be steadfast and unmovable—always abounding in the work of the LORD. This is the year to open our mouths to cry aloud and spare not. We must take authority, dominion, and power.

Decree and declare the aforementioned declarations over your family and loved ones, today. In Jesus' authority, I pray. Amen!

> "I am the Lord thy God, which brought thee out of the land of Egypt: open thy mouth wide, and I will fill it."
>
> — PSALMS 81:10 (KJV)

You have a choice– either you can speak life or you can speak death over yourself. What choice will you make today? You also have another choice. You can ask God to help you to apply His principles, regarding management and stewardship, to become prosperous in this land. Remember, God supplies all your needs, and you must learn the Word, therefore, being able to put a demand on the Word of God – supply and demand.

Will you consider receiving salvation or re-commitment of your life today? I want to encourage you in the hope of the Lord. I'm leaving you with Romans 12:10-19.

> Be kindly affectioned one to another with brotherly love; in honor preferring one another; Not slothful in business; fervent in spirit; serving the Lord; Rejoicing

> in hope; patient in tribulation; continuing instant in prayer; Distributing to the necessity of saints; given to hospitality. Bless them which persecute you: bless, and curse not. Rejoice with them that do rejoice, and weep with them that weep. Be of the same mind one toward another. Mind not high things, but condescend to men of low estate. Be not wise in your own conceits. Recompense to no man evil for evil. Provide things honest in the sight of all men. If it be possible, as much as lieth in you, live peaceably with all men. Dearly beloved, avenge not yourselves, but rather give place unto wrath: for it is written, Vengeance is mine; I will repay, saith the Lord.
>
> — ROMANS 12:10-19 (KJV)

Prayer for Supply and Demand

Help me to make good, sound, and strategic decisions. Lord, help me to cut away the things I want but do not need. Help me to persevere in this season and be content with what I have for you alone to supply my every need. I thank You for safety, protection, provision, and vision.

We come humbly before Your throne of grace and mercy on this day, God, to say thank You. Thank You for being our Sovereign God. You are the supreme authority and all things are under Your control. You are the creator of the whole universe. And we humble ourselves before you, Lord. You are the owner of heaven and earth.

We thank You that You have full right and power of the governing body over itself, without interference from any outside sources or bodies. We thank You, God, that Your characteristics don't change. You are the Holy Spirit— infinite in all Your ways, eternal, never-ending, and unchangeable in who You are. You are full of wisdom, power, holiness, justice, goodness, and truth.

God, we thank You for Your words. God, we thank You that You are our supply and demand, resource, and source. Jesus, thank You for always having our best interest at heart. Help us to be content with You and You alone. Lord, give us wisdom for wisdom comes from You. Help us to be accountable for our decisions. Help us to make good, sound, and strategic decisions. Lord, help us to cut away the things we desire and want. Help us to be content with what we have for You alone supply our every need. We thank You for safety, protection, provision, and vision.

We thank You that You are omnipotent— You have all power. God, You do whatever you want. God, You are not subject to physical limitations like man. Being omnipotent, You have power over wind, water, gravity, physics, and the like. God, Your power is infinite and limitless.

We thank You that You are omniscient— all-knowing. You are aware of the past, present, and future. Nothing takes You by surprise. Your knowledge is total and complete. You know all that there is to know and all that can be known.

We thank You that You are omnipresent— always present. God, You are capable of being everywhere at the same time. Your divine presence encompasses the whole of the universe. There is no location You do not inhabit.

Let us not be confused with pantheism, which suggests that You are synonymous with the universe itself; instead, omnipresence indicates that You, God, are distinct from the universe, but inhabit the entirety of it. You are everywhere! These three attributes and characteristics are the essentials of Your nature.

We adore You, God. We magnify You, God. We lift You high with our worship and our praise. It is You, God, who is pulling us through. It is You, God, that supplies every one of our needs. It is You, God, who causes us to rise every morning with new grace, mercy, unspeakable joy, peace that surpasses all understanding, wisdom, clarity, and a sound mind— with the ability and authority to speak, decree, declare, and put a demand on the Word of God.

We thank You, God, for the family bonds. We thank You for our youth generation. We thank You that our government and world leaders are putting You back in Your rightful place, sitting high upon Your throne— high above the highest of heavens. Let men bow down and worship You, our one and only true and living God! We ask You for the forgiveness of our sins with a pure and clean heart. Father God, make us clean inside!

We thank You for endowing us with financial wisdom, allowing us to create kingdom wealth, and standing on your Word and Your promises. Father God, we humbly ask for forgiveness if we have sinned against Thee in any way, knowingly or unknowingly. We repent of our sins and ask that You accept our repentance prayers as restitution of our land. We thank You that the healing process has already begun. Help us to remember "The Lord's Prayer" in the book of Matthew in the sixth chapter. It says that you forgive our trespasses, as we forgive those who trespass against us, not those who have apologized to us.

So, God, we ask that Your Holy Spirit come and saturate this room today. Holy Spirit, You are welcome to have Your way. We thank You, God, that You are our supplier, and You demand us to repent our sins. As You hear our prayers, we ask that You have mercy upon the universe and bring us back into right standing before You.

We ask these prayers and the unspoken prayers of our hearts to reach heaven and help us to embrace our new normal. Help us be radically obedient to Your covenant Commandments, and love You first with all of our heart, mind, body, and soul. Help us love our neighbors, as we love ourselves.

We ask that these prayers manifest in the earth, and that not one of our petitions come back void. We stand on Your Word. We stand on Your promises. We believe in and receive Your healing virtues. Holy Spirit, increase in me and flow through me. Open our eyes, ears, and hearts to hear what the Lord says. We will be ever so careful to give You all the worship, honor, and praise.

In Jesus' mighty Authority, we pray. Amen.

* * *

8

SAVING MONEY GOD'S WAY

Most of our parents are good savers and are very resourceful. They know how to work the grounds, plant seeds, and await the harvest to feed the family and sometimes others in the community. My father was a stickler for saving, considering he lived through the "Great Depression."

From the age of 12, I worked at my family's fish market, called Ashland Seafood. Whenever I got paid (in cash), my father would take me straight to the bank. He would make me save 50% of my paycheck since I was living at home with no bills. With the other 50%, I was able to buy clothes, shoes, entertainment, fast food, and other personal items. My father even had me buy my senior class ring. It wasn't because he couldn't afford it, but it was because he was teaching me responsibility and accountability. This was like clockwork; every week, I was made to put half of my earrings in a savings account. There was no room for excuses, like saying, "I forgot." My father watched over me as an eagle watches over her eaglets.

Most people today do not save anything from their present income. This means that people in this generation are saving 0% of their income. It also means that they are squandering their savings on daily entertainment and other expenditures. It's imperative to exercise discipline in budgeting and learn how to pay ourselves at least 10% of the income received.

It's important that you start somewhere in your saving process. Your children are watching you closely to see how efficient you are in balancing your household income and how responsible you are in paying your creditors. Individuals who save none of their income are probably suffering from the "I gotta have it" or "I want it now" syndrome. This mindset can be changed, through planning and an accountability partner. Learn to be intentional on purpose to fulfill your goal of budgeting and becoming debt-free. Patience is not always easy when your income is less than the amount needed to pay your household expenses.

Be Patient

Learning to wait on things and being cheerful about the wait is a taught behavior. Individuals who didn't learn this behavior growing up have experienced some real negative situations, as adults in the area of finance and credit. My goal for writing this book is to provide the tools necessary to become financially literate and fiscally fit. My goal is to provide insight that pertains to budgeting so that it will be passed down from generation to generation for the fulfillment of knowledge, understanding, and wisdom in the area of finance, economic growth and development.

God tends to ration out His blessing slowly upon you. This is a way to keep you humble and to remind you of your dependence on Him. It also encourages one to be thankful for what God has already done, including the little things. This reaffirms your need for His guidance and blessings. You should not be frugal with your finances and resources, but rather gather over time. It's a time to show forth maturity in the area of finance.

God can send large amounts of money into your hands, suddenly. God is strategic in His actions and will trickle in wealth. Why would God do this? He does this to teach you and me self-discipline and self-control. With these two attributes, we can have a long-term plan in place to build our family's financial strength, instead of being so quick to splurge on things that do not add any value to us or our overall legacy. He who gathers money little by little makes it grow (Proverbs 13:11). Those get-rich-quick schemes are just what they mean. Many are losing money in the bitcoin stock and other investments that promise a return on funds invested within a short period of time. You have seen those who win millions in the lottery, and just a few years later, they have nothing of value to show where their money disappeared. If you fail to plan, you plan to fail. One must learn to manage well with the resources provided.

Manage Your Risk

> "The poor are always ruled over by the rich, so don't borrow and put yourself under their power."
>
> — PROVERBS 22:7 (MSG)

The first decade of the 21st century was, for certain, a miserable financial experience for consumers, banks, and the housing market. People were gambling too much money on new internet stocks, resulting in the market crashing; and this affected me personally as a mortgage loan officer, during this era. I would advise my clients away from adjustable-rate mortgage loans, interest-only loans, balloon loans, and No Document/ No Money Down loans. There were many unethical loan officers who didn't care about their clients' long-term needs, as they were only concerned with lining their pockets and getting richer – so they thought. Some mortgage loan officers failed to educate their clients on the products and operations, so they approved individuals for these types of loans, like children in a candy store. The proper presentation of different loan products was never properly presented to the client; therefore, the client wasn't able to make a strategic decision and manage the risks of the decisions. As a result, clients lost their homes, due to foreclosure and the inability to pay off their debts.

Truth be told, there are many components that go into a mortgage process. One of the most important ones is your debt-to-income ratios. I know this might sound foreign to some of you; so, let me break this down for you. Debt-to-income ratios can make or break your loan application. The lenders add all your income versus all your debt that is paid out monthly. Then, they divide the two and come up with your debt-to-income ratios. The ideal ratio is 38% debt to 28% income. Lenders want to make sure you have the ability to repay the mortgage. If your debt is over 40%, it is considered a slight risk. If you have an outstanding credit score of 750 or above, there's a chance you will still be approved for the loan, provided you present the underwriter with a letter of explanation (LOX). Providing the LOX with as much detail about your specific situation is a benefit, not a hindrance. This letter will give the underwriter insight into your specific situation. Lower credit scores will ensure that you will be denied the credit, due to late payments, missed monthly payments, collections, and charge-offs.

What's the point here? Watch what you do. Weigh the decisions you are making; and do your homework before making any type of purchase. Work the numbers into your prepared budget. Be sure to read the fine print, and don't allow anyone to pressure you into purchasing. Keep your exposure to risk as low as possible. Never forget this statement: "The borrower is servant to the lender" (Proverbs 22:7 KJV). The more debt you accumulate, the more of a slave you become to your indebtedness. It's important for you to have some connections in the finance and credit industry. You all have me. I come with over 30 years of experience in this industry. I have also counseled hundreds of clients, helping them purchase their own homes successfully— and they are still in them today! I have been successful in aiding my clients to improve their overall credit scores and FICO scores, to become "A" Paper ready (a 700 credit score or higher). I also negotiate with creditors to settle or remove collections, liens, and tax levies, as the client and I work on improving their overall financial portfolio.

Time is of the essence. Think about what it is you need first, as it's about prioritizing your life. Look at the examples of others, and learn from others' mistakes. Some lessons in life can be learned through others' experiences and not your own. Think about how this is going to affect your family. Now, talk to God about everything you have pondered over in your mind, and listen for strategy or direction.

Pay Your Debt

> "Never walk away from someone who deserves help; your hand is God's hand for that person. Don't tell your neighbor 'Maybe some other time' or 'Try me tomorrow' when the money's right there in your pocket. Don't figure [out] ways of taking advantage of your neighbor when he's sitting there trusting and unsuspecting."
>
> — PROVERBS 3:27-29 (MSG)

Have you ever heard of the generational theory? The concept of the generational theory is that there are very different cultures, including money cultures, depending on how old you are now. People from the Great Depression or World War II generation, who were known as the "builders," hated debt; but millennials today tend to not worry about borrowing. "Builders" paid with cash, while millennials usually go get another credit card or request another loan.

When it comes to borrowing, the "builders" were wiser in their decision-making process. Every financial planner who truly cares about the needs of their clients will encourage and advise their clients to pay down their debt, as soon as possible. They say this because interest payments eat away at cash-on-hand. For example, if I am only paying interest only, I am never paying anything toward my principal balance. So, a good rule of thumb is to make sure you pay more than just the interest each month or the minimum payment due each month. Try to pay additional principal, whenever it is feasible; you will save on the back end and pay off debt quicker.

Out-of-control debt also destroys our credit rating and makes it extremely hard to get a decent loan and interest rate on important things (like a home or a car). Paying your debt down rapidly also applies to those personal loans and loans acquired through friends or family members. Proverbs 3:28 says, "Don't say to your neighbor, 'Come back tomorrow, and I'll give it to you' – when you already have it with you" (NIV). Remember, lending should be made from your overflow of funds, not your necessity. This is good financial advice, and it may even help save a friendship or a family relationship when lending from your surplus.

The Art of Budgeting is a great tool for any household, especially when it comes to accessing your income and expenses. This is an opportunity to see, on paper, a clear, financial picture of all that makes up your household.

Leave an Estate/ Inheritance

> "A good man leaveth an inheritance to his children's children: and the wealth of the sinner is laid up for the just."
>
> — PROVERBS 13:22 (KJV)

Do you have an insurance policy? If so, who are you covering on the insurance policy? Do you have your beneficiaries updated? Do you have a will/living will or last will and testament? These are all some important questions you and your family need to address. I would venture to say that over half of the world's population will die intestate.

What does the word "intestate" mean? It means that there is no written or living will or last will and testament. If you die without a will, the state will then take control of your estate and make all the decisions, regarding the disposition of your property and other final values. The state will then charge your estate for its services.

A Living Will or Last Will of Testament

Have you planned for your last will and testament? Why, or why not? Procrastination is the number one reason why many have not put these documents in order. People say they will deal with this matter someday, but the reality is that some never do. Although you have good intentions, this can get lost in your day-to-day shuffle when not properly planned. Oftentimes, some people think: "When I'm dead, it won't matter anyway." Maybe, some people have a phobia about death and hate to even think about it. Either way, it is important to your children and grandchildren to be specific in planning the dissolution of your estate. If you have no children, it is still important to name a successor or a responsible person to be the executor of the estate. When it comes to inheritance, one family member may feel like they are entitled to it as opposed to the other, sometimes leaving many family relationships severed, without repair.

God loves it when His children plan ahead and manage the things He has blessed us with. According to Proverbs 13:22, God absolutely loves it when people plan to take care of generations to come.

A monetary blessing left for our children and grandchildren could help them purchase their own homes. It can not only be a big investment in them but also for future generations. It has the potential to change their status from renters to homeowners, help a grandchild go to college, help relieve a surmountable debt that has accumulated over time, or even help start a self-made business. God has given us such a great heritage from those who have gone on before us, and it is a blessing to bestow it to our future generation, as a way to show gratitude.

Remember to make that budget, stick to the plan, manage the risk, pay off debt (as quickly as possible), and most of all, leave an inheritance to your children and grandchildren.

> True humility and fear of the Lord lead to riches, honor, and long life.
>
> — PROVERBS 22:4 NLT

Prayer Over Household Blessing

Father God, thank You for being a good Father. Thank You for every good and perfect gift. Thank You, God, that You provide for all of our needs, according to Your riches in glory. Thank You that all of our needs are met. Thank You, God, that You give us a "yes" and "amen."

Matthew 18:18 says, "Whatever you bind on earth will be bound in heaven, and whatever you loose on earth will be loosed in heaven" (NIV). Therefore, I bind up the poverty mindset and release prosperity to every reader. I bind up lack and release the abundance of rain and overflow of prosperity in health and wealth. I bind up distractions, and I release clarity of thoughts in the mind. I bind up depression and anxiety and release your peace that surpasses all understanding.

For God, You said in Your Word that when we are weak, that is when Your Holy Spirit is made strong within us. Your joy is our strength, so strengthen us today. Let joy flow, like a river, overflowing its banks.

Father, I bind up procrastination and release enthusiasm and a proactive attitude when it comes to taking care of the business in my household. Although the enemy's plan is to deceive, God, You said, "No weapon formed against [us] shall prosper, and every tongue which rises up against [us] in judgment You shall condemn. This is [our inheritance]" (Isaiah 54:17 NKJV). God, we depend on You to see us through every trial, tribulation, hurt, betrayal, and all matters of the heart.

Transform our hearts and lives, Lord. Transform us from the inside out. God, thank You in advance for the many blessings that You have already supplied. Thank You, God, for loving us enough to prepare us for the release of Your transfer of wealth and riches. Thank You, God, for wisdom, knowledge, and understanding.

Father, as I close this prayer, keep the minds of my family, children, and loved ones focused, following one course until successful. Give us the ability to stay committed, be consistent, and start using the tools to prepare the budget, which will help to transform our lives, forever. Father God, help each reader to leave a legacy and an inheritance to their children.

In Jesus' mighty Name, we pray. Amen.

* * *

9

IDENTITY THEFT (BONUS CHAPTER)

VOLUME 2: TAKE OWNERSHIP

America is currently experiencing enormous reports of identity theft. With scammers and identity thieves operating across the globe, nations are experiencing problems. The advancement of technology has been revolutionizing the world. As a result, most consumers have shifted to buying and selling things online, which has added to the identity theft crisis. Many small business owners and entrepreneurs have not been able to recover. The "mom-and-pop" business is almost a thing of the past.

People who steal others' identities will use your credit score, bank accounts, social security number, and your assets. They use the things you have worked hard to achieve through self-control and self-discipline. As a result, they try to live a life that is not true to them, but rather to you.

As a result of worrying too much about what other people think rather than what God thinks, you adopt the identities of the people you read about, see on television, or follow on social media, rather than remaining true to yourself. Worrying about other people's acceptance of you is one of the greatest strongholds to overcome. What is the cause of this stronghold?

The Word of God helps us understand this more clearly. In

Galatians 1, we read about the religious leaders called Judaizers who sought to place believers under a performance standard "under the law," thereby abandoning grace. In Galatians 1:10, Paul talks about these well-meaning, Bible-quoting leaders who were ripping the saints off and pulling them away from God's grace. Paul says, "Am I now seeking the faith of man or God? Or am I serving to please men? If I were still trying to please men, I would not be a bond-servant of Christ" (Galatians 1:10). Paul is saying that it is possible to be more people-orientated than God-orientated. In Proverbs 29:25 (NASB), it says, "The fear of man brings a snare, but he who trusts in the Lord will be exalted." Satan uses your legitimate need for acceptance in an illegitimate way, resulting in you living under a false identity.

Pay attention. You'll notice how confused people are when they try to please everyone. One minute they are pleasing one person, and the next minute, they are pleasing someone else. These people must be around others who make them feel good; otherwise, they become depressed. These people are called people-pleasers. How do you begin to overcome these strongholds of worrying about what others think? It is when you decide what God says about you that matters most.

Know what God has for you; His plan is designed, specifically and especially, for you. God doesn't give your blessings to others. He prepares you for the blessing that He has in store for you by taking you through the process. He matures you, as a Believer, so that you no longer need milk, but can eat meat instead. Despite your ugly tears, messed-up hair days, days without make-up, and rants, God still loves you! If you allow yourself to be driven by people's approval, just remember, people are fallible, and their emotions shift. Your identity determines your destiny. So, you must protect your identity, both naturally and spiritually– which brings me to our next point of reference. Do you know what to do if you are a victim of identity theft?

Five Steps to Take When You Are a Victim of Identity Theft

1) *File an initial fraud alert/ file with one agency.* The agency you select will report that information to the other two agencies. It's normally free to file. The three major credit reporting agencies you can use are Experian, Equifax, and TransUnion.

2) *Initiate a credit freeze.* This denies anyone from looking up your credit. If you want to know how long the freeze can stay on your credit report, contact your state's attorney general's office. This is generally free to victims of identity theft. If there is a fee, it's normally a small fee, like $10. Place alerts on the three credit reporting agencies, previously mentioned, and request a copy of your credit report when filing the fraud alert. This is free to victims of fraud and identity theft. Look over each report in detail to see what is not yours.

3. *File an identity theft report with local authorities and the federal agency.* The report helps you get fraudulent information removed from your credit report, which stops businesses and collections agencies from coming after you for debts that are not yours.

> Filing a report is a two-part process. The *Federal Trade Commission* is a government agency that helps protect you, the consumer, from fraud. You can file this report online at https://reportfraud.ftc.gov/#/ and complete your report. After completing your report, you will be issued an FTC Identity Theft Affidavit. Print this report, and keep it for your records.
>
> Then, you will need to file a police report in person, or you may be able to do this online. Check with your local police department for instructions and the items you will need to file the report for proof of your identity. After filing a police report, ask for a copy of the report and the filing number.

> After completing the FTC Affidavit and obtaining a police report filing number, you have a complete identity theft report. Now, you are ready to take on each fraudulent item that you may have discovered in your credit report.

4. *Contact credit bureaus, lenders, and businesses, and file a dispute with the fraud department of each company and each credit reporting agency.* While this may be time-consuming, it's important for you to take good notes and keep all records. Make note of their names, the date, and the time you spoke with them, and write down any instructions given by the fraud department. The FTC has many helpful resources, and they provide a checklist for how to dispute different claims.

> (If you desire assistance, contact us via website: www.trifold-connectionsllc.com, email: info@trifoldconnectionsllc.com, or phone 708-553-0002)

5. *Place an extended fraud alert on file with each reporting credit agency.* This alert is free and lasts for seven years. It allows you to receive two free credit reports a year to stay on top of any new or suspicious activity. Also, during this time of the health crisis, the FTC website allows monthly reports for no additional charge. There are more than the three major credit reporting agencies; so, check your local listings for other reporting agencies and contact them, as well.

You Gamble on Life, So Gamble on God

In these times, God's people must trust Him to rest their bodies, minds, and souls. When you choose to trust God (rather than trying to please God), you enter into the realm of faith, believing in what cannot be seen; yet, acting as if you can see it. It's a gamble!

> Now, faith is confidence in what we hope for and assurance about what we do not see.
>
> — HEBREWS 11:1 NIV

Your identity and positioning in Christ are unseen in the physical world. In fact, the world screams out the opposite, telling you that you are a failure, guilty, and inadequate. It takes real faith to act on God's proclamation that you are accepted, forgiven, and complete in Christ. Yes, faith is putting your trust in Him, and what He says is true. Faith is putting your lives in His hands, even though you can't see or trace Him.

> "By faith, we understand that the universe was formed at God's command, so that what is seen was not made out of what was visible.
>
> — HEBREWS 11:3 NIV

The physical evidence for God's creation is conclusive; yet, it still takes faith for you and me to believe that God created the universe because we weren't there to see it happen. I also believe it takes faith to believe that God has made you new creatures in Christ! Anyone who comes to Christ must believe that He exists and that He rewards those who earnestly seek Him (Hebrews 11:6).

Blaise Pascal, the famous French philosopher, physicist, and mathematician put it this way, "Belief is a wise wager. Granted that faith cannot be proved, what harm will come to you if you gamble on its truth, and it proves false? If you gain, you gain all; if you lose, you lose nothing. Wager, then, without hesitation, that He exists."

The God Who Cares

God hears you when you pray. It's that simple and that profound. Unless you sit in this truth, you will miss how incredible and life-altering this is.

In 1 Peter 5, the disciple Peter tells us to humble ourselves before the Lord and to cast our cares upon Him. He explains that we have an adversary who is attacking us and that Believers throughout the world are suffering. In the seventh verse, he tells us to cast our cares upon the Lord, because He cares for us.

How often do we take this for granted? Of course, He cares for us, but think about it for a moment. Why should He? Don't forget, the same Bible that makes this statement also tells us that all human beings have rejected God (Romans 1), that everyone has sinned and refuses to seek after God (Romans 3), and that we are all dead in our sins (Ephesians 2). There is no logical step between "we have all rejected him" and "He cares for us all." And yet, there it is– illogical but real.

Consider this statement, "God cares for you." So, cast your cares upon Him, and lay every burden down at His feet. He cares about you and wants to hear what's concerning you. It's that simple, but this simple realization will change your life. Let it! Right this second, God is listening to you and me. Because He cares, He hears. He's listening and waiting to hear your voice, so say something to Him. Practice believing that He is listening and cares what we will say. Then, say something– anything– because He hears.

Prayer Of Our True Identity

Before we pray concerning our true identity, let's examine the Word of God in Matthew.

The World Is Not A Stage

> "Be especially careful when you are trying to be good so that you don't make a performance out of it. It might be good theater, but the God who made you won't be applauding.
>
> When you do something for someone else, don't call attention to yourself. You've seen them in action, I'm sure—"playactors" I call them—treating prayer meeting and street corner alike as a stage, acting compassionate as long as someone is watching, playing to the crowds. They get applause, true, but that's all they get. When you help someone out, don't

think about how it looks. Just do it—quietly and unobtrusively. That is the way your God, who conceived you in love, working behind the scenes, helps you out.

— MATTHEW 6:1-4 MSG

Pray With Simplicity

"And when you come before God, don't turn that into a theatrical production either. All these people making a regular show out of their prayers, hoping for fifteen minutes of fame! Do you think God sits in a box seat?

Here's what I want you to do: Find a quiet, secluded place so you won't be tempted to role-play before God. Just be there as simply and honestly as you can manage. The focus will shift from you to God, and you will begin to sense his grace.

The world is full of so-called prayer warriors who are prayer-ignorant. They're full of formulas and programs and advice, peddling techniques for getting what you want from God. Don't fall for that nonsense. This is your Father you are dealing with, and he knows better than you what you need. With a God like this loving you, you can pray very simply. Like this:

Our Father in heaven,
Reveal who you are.
Set the world right;
Do what's best—
as above, so below.
Keep us alive with three square meals.
Keep us forgiven with you and forgiving others.
Keep us safe from ourselves and the Devil.
You're in charge!

You can do anything you want!
You're ablaze in beauty!
Yes. Yes. Yes.

In prayer there is a connection between what God does and what you do. You can't get forgiveness from God, for instance, without also forgiving others. If you refuse to do your part, you cut yourself off from God's part.

When you practice some appetite-denying discipline to better concentrate on God, don't make a production out of it. It might turn you into a small-time celebrity but it won't make you a saint. If you "go into training" inwardly, act normal outwardly. Shampoo and comb your hair, brush your teeth, wash your face. God doesn't require attention-getting devices. He won't overlook what you are doing; he'll reward you well.

— MATTHEW 6:5-18 MSG

* * *

Dear God, I believe that You exist. I believe that by trusting You, I am pleasing You. Today, by the promise of Your Holy Spirit, my counselor, I choose to believe what You say is true about me. I am loved, adopted, accepted, chosen, appointed, anointed, and cherished by You in and through Christ Jesus!

Father God, protect our identities from falling victim to the world's systems/technology. With new technology developing daily, Father, help us to protect our identities and the identity of our family members and loved ones.

Help us, Father, to embrace our true identities in Christ Jesus. Help us not to be ashamed of who we are. Help us stand boldly in our faith, proclaiming Your good news and promises of 'yes' and 'amen' in our lives! Increase our wisdom, knowledge, and understanding; increase our ability to exercise self-discipline and self-control.

Keep us FOCUSed (Following One Course Until Successful). Continue to cut away the things and obstacles in our lives that keep us from growing and maturing in our kingdom walk and assignments.

I break off any chains of bondage keeping us in a poverty mindset. I decree and declare financial wealth, and a sound mind to make difficult decisions concerning investing in ourselves and into the kingdom of God.

I decree and declare that we will become fiscally fit and use our time, talents, and treasures in building up God's kingdom here on earth. I release an overflow of creativity in the hearts and minds of God's people. I release a servant's heart. You said in your Word that if we want to be first, we must become the last or the least of them, serving one another in spirit and in truth, loving one another to wholeness.

God, allow humility, integrity, character, overflow, and abundance to be our portion. God, we have taken a gamble on many things in this world. Now, allow us to take a gamble on You. For You said in Your Word that we are winners, overcomers, conquerors, and victors.

We trust You even when we can't trace You, and love our enemies as we do ourselves. We thank You, God, that You care for us and desire to see us prosper spiritually, physically, emotionally, and financially. You help us to be good stewards of the many blessings You have already bestowed upon us and the many blessings still to come.

God, You want us to know that You hear our prayers and that You listen to every word that comes out of our mouths, even the unspoken words of our hearts. You transform our hearts and heal us in our broken areas. You desire to have an intimate relationship with us. So, we put all of our hearts' concerns on the altar before You to work it out! We know that You love and care for us, no matter our status, addictions, unhealthy habits, unworthiness, or brokenness. God, You always meet us right where we are.

Your Word says, "My grace is sufficient for you, for my power is made perfect in weakness" (2 Corinthians 12:9 KJV). Everyone who is born of flesh and blood is weak, but not everyone is aware of their weaknesses because they are not God-fearing. Help us, God, to humble ourselves before You and proclaim to a dying world that You are Lord!

I ask, God, that You cover these prayers in Your Son Jesus' Blood of the New Covenant, letting our requests be known unto You, God, who is the author and finisher of our faith.

In Jesus' mighty Authority, we pray. Amen.

* * *

FINAL THOUGHTS FROM THE AUTHOR

The money you manage isn't really your money, you know!? It's God's money. So, I encourage you to remember, "To whom much is given, much is required."

Can God trust you with your wealth?

ABOUT THE AUTHOR

Henrietta England is an esteemed financial service consultant who has found much success at Trifold Connections LLC. She began her career in 1983 as a customer service representative and credit consultant for the Nelson Brothers Furniture Company. Soon thereafter, she garnered over 10 years of experience as a senior banker and mortgage loan officer at LaSalle Bank and Bank of America. Prior to her current role, she excelled as the Vice President and Branch Manager at Standard Bank and Trust.

Currently, she manages the day-to-day functions at Tri Fold Connections LLC. She produces weekly broadcasts within her "Money Matters Mondays" series, which are educational programs that can be viewed virtually on YouTube, LinkedIn, Twitter, Facebook, Twitch, and her website.

Henrietta truly enjoys educating others to help them move forward to financial freedom, abundance, and overflow. She utilizes Biblical principles and precepts in financial literacy, economic growth, and development to help individuals build kingdom wealth, God's way!

youtube.com/@trifoldconnections3835

www.ingramcontent.com/pod-product-compliance
Lightning Source LLC
Chambersburg PA
CBHW041300210926
51847CB00009B/92
9781955297325